"Daniel Carr and M̶ lent Advent devotic ment passages into a tapestry of truth that celebrates the revealing of the Lord Jesus. This is a refreshing read for the entire family, and it is certain to become a cherished part of Christmas celebrations for generations to come."

Dr. John Yeats
Executive Director
Missouri Baptist Convention

"Carr and Winslow offer a gift to families: twenty-five daily readings to help situate the birth of the Messiah in the larger story of Israel. Families will discover parallels between Jesus' birth and six other births to women previously experiencing infertility. With the help of guiding questions at the conclusion of each day, this study reinforces that the unchanging God of Abraham, Isaac, and Jacob is none other than God the Father of Jesus."

Dr. Matthew C. Easter
Director of Christian Studies
Missouri Baptist University

"*The Seventh Birthday* presents a holistic portrait of Christ that will stir your affections for Immanuel, God with us. The metanarrative of Scripture comes alive as the authors trace six unlikely births in Scripture and show how all six point to Christ. This is a wonderful, Gospel-saturated family resource that will help orient your hearts to the Savior this Advent!"

Heather Kauffman
Author of *The Story People* and *Loving Isaac*

"Daniel Carr and Martin Winslow have uniquely tapped into the richness of Holy Scripture through the stories of the Old Testament and Gospels to deliver to us this Advent resource. Our hearts will be greatly stirred and warmed as we walk through the stories of these characters and see Christ at every turn. I wholeheartedly recommend you consider the use of this valuable tool for this year, and for Christmases to come."

Dr. Rick Hedger
Director, Multiplying Churches
Missouri Baptist Convention

"In an age in which the Old Testament has been challenged with regard to relevance and importance, *The Seventh Birthday* masterfully and devotionally demonstrates the intrinsic connection between the Old and New. Readers will come away with a fresh sense of God's love, God's forgiveness, and God's sovereignty. Moreover, readers will find themselves called to a greater and truer hope in the gospel of Jesus."

Mark Lanting, Ed.D.
Dean of Communications & Humanities
Rock Valley College

THE SEVENTH BIRTHDAY

An Advent Devotional for Families

MARTIN WINSLOW
DANIEL CARR

Foreword by
PROFESSOR STEPHEN J. ANDREWS

high street press

Editors: Brianna Boes, Rob Phillips
Cover design: Laura Schembre
Chapter Illustrations: Chloe Boes
Layout: Brianna Boes
Kindle production: Brianna Boes

High Street Press is the publishing arm of the Missouri Baptist Convention (MBC) and exists because of the generous support of Missouri Baptists through the Cooperative Program. To learn more about High Street Press and its resources, visit highstreet.press. To learn more about the MBC and the way its 1,800 affiliated churches cooperate voluntarily for the sake of the gospel, visit mobaptist.org.

We would like to dedicate this Advent devotional to every couple struggling through the pain of infertility. Don't give up hope in the God that opens the womb.

"He makes the barren woman abide in the house as a joyful mother of children. Praise the Lord!"
Psalm 113:9

CONTENTS

FOREWORD

BY PROFESSOR STEPHEN J. ANDREWS

Baptists have not been very keen on following the Christian calendar like most liturgical churches. Epiphany, Ash Wednesday, and Lent are not common terms in their jargon. On the other hand, two events in the Christian calendar, Christmas and Easter, are considered to be of great importance to Baptist faith. Both events recount a vital part of the gospel story.

Baptists celebrate Christmas in different ways. Some churches follow the Advent season as Christmastide; some do not. It is not unusual to encounter Advent traditions in many churches: hanging of the greens, Chrismon trees, Advent wreaths, and Advent candles. On each of the Advent Sundays selected, church families come to the front of the church to light an Advent candle and remind the church of the coming of the Christ child. Advent celebrates both the first coming of Jesus as a child in the nativity of Bethlehem and the second coming of Jesus as the risen Savior.

The Seventh Birthday provides an important tool to recognize the meaning and power of Advent. The book's purpose is to offer church families and individual believers a personal plan to celebrate the coming of the Christ child. The authors' study helps place the birth of our Savior within the rich tapestry of God's redemptive history, starting in the Old Testament and leading up to the fulfillment of the Messiah's birth in the City of David.

Rather than investigate prophetic predictions and well-known theological themes concerning the coming of the Savior – important as these are, indeed – Martin Winslow and Daniel Carr trace the hand of God in six miraculous births occurring prior to the advent of the Messiah. Each of these six births involved mothers giving birth in difficult circumstances. Each of these mothers were barren, unable to conceive. Nevertheless, through the great faith of these women and God's divine mercy and intervention, each was able to bear a son who had a great impact on the people of God.

Not only did the miraculous pregnancies foreshadow the virgin conception of Mary, the six sons served "as precursors to Christ through their unique gifts, characteristics, and stories." The births of the six men – Isaac, Jacob, Joseph, Samson, Samuel, and John the Baptist – pointed the way to "the seventh birthday," the last miraculous birth recorded in the Bible. Each of these men revealed "shadows of the Messiah who is to come."

The Seventh Birthday provides a reading for every day of the Advent season. Families participate in the readings by lighting candles, answering questions, investigating suggested Scripture passages, singing carols, and offering a prayer for each day. Following the readings and the recommended procedures deepens your faith and the faith of your family. It will surely help you recognize God's divine plan of salvation that began at creation and was brought to fruition in the birth of Christ, the cross of Calvary, and the empty tomb.

Above all, this book helps you appreciate more deeply the meaning of Christmas and heighten your anticipation and excitement in the true purpose of Advent: to celebrate the first coming of our Savior as a baby in a manger, and to long for the second coming of our risen Savior! Maranatha, Lord Jesus!

Stephen J. Andrews
Senior Professor of Hebrew and Old Testament
Midwestern Baptist Theological Seminary
Senior Pastor
Providence Baptist Church, Kansas City

INTRODUCTION

The end of December is the time that Christians celebrate the miraculous birthday of our Messiah, Jesus. But what if we told you there were six other special births that came before the birth of Jesus which helped prepare the world for the most miraculous birthday ever?

Let me explain.

Themes emerge throughout the Old Testament that are eventually fulfilled in the New Testament, specifically in the person of Jesus. A perfect example of this is the theme of atonement we see in the sacrificial system. The entire system existed to teach us why we needed Jesus, "the lamb of God who takes away the sin of the world" (Jn. 1:29). The sacrificial system was weak and continuous; there was no sacrifice that could cover all sin, not even all sin for one person (Heb. 10:1-4). The system was meant to point to the one who would put an end to sacrifice. At the cross, Jesus said, "It is finished" (Jn. 19:30). After he "had made purification of sins" through his death, he "sat down at the right hand of the Majesty on high" (Heb 1:3) and fulfilled the purpose of the sacrificial system that had been so ingrained into the very fabric of Judaism. "For by one offering He has perfected for all time those who are sanctified" (Heb. 10:14).

The theme we are going to look at in this book is the theme of miraculous birth as seen first in the births of six men born to six previously barren women and then, finally, as seen in the birth of Jesus Christ to the virgin Mary. When examined closely, the births and lives of these first six men reveal shadows of the Messiah who is to come.

The first six women we will look at during our journey toward Bethlehem will all be referred to as barren. Whereas we may use the word *barren* to refer to a woman who cannot conceive, it seems as though these particular women are barren because of God's will. The Hebrew word for *barren* is *acar*, and the word is tied to divine activity when attributed to women of the Old Testament.[1] Every time *acar* occurs in the Bible, God must intervene to make conception a reality. These women and their miraculous pregnancies foreshadow the virgin Mary. Likewise, their six sons serve as precursors to Christ through their unique gifts, characteristics, and stories.

We have included a chart detailing a few commonalities between the births of these six sons and the birth of Jesus, who was born of a virgin. Jesus's birth is the seventh and last miraculous birth recorded in Scripture. This book provides a reading for every day of the Advent season, including Christmas Day. You will spend three days on each special, Old Covenant family. The readings over the last seven days will demonstrate how Jesus is the fulfillment of our chosen scriptural theme. Light a candle for each miraculous birth as you read with your family. Add a candle every three days until the nineteenth day. Then for the next seven days, light seven candles each day during the reading in honor of the coming of Jesus. After each chapter, there are some songs to sing and practical questions for families to work through together as you ponder the miracles of God. And when you are finished, have a very merry Christmas!

Parents	Problem of Barrenness	Divine Announcement/ Promise	Promise Comes to Fruition	Result
1) Abraham & Sarah, old people	Genesis 11:29	Genesis 18:10	Genesis 21:1-2	Isaac, Initiation of Old Covenant
2) Isaac & Rebekah	Genesis 25:21	Genesis 25:23	Genesis 25:24	Jacob
3) Jacob & Rachel	Genesis 29:31	Genesis 30:22	Genesis 30:23-24	Joseph
4) Manoah & Wife	Judges 13:2	Judges 13:3	Judges 13:24	Samson
5) Elkanah & Hannah	1 Samuel 1:6, 2:5	1 Samuel 1:19	1 Samuel 1:19	Samuel
6) Zacharias & Elizabeth, old people	Luke 1:7	Luke 1:13	Luke 1:57	John, finality of Old Covenant
7) Joseph & Mary, young/new people	Luke 1:27, the anomaly of virginity	Luke 1:31	Luke 2:7	Jesus, the New Covenant

PART ONE

Isaac the Sacrifice

ISAAC THE SACRIFICE
OLD PEOPLE HAVING CHILDREN?

December 1st
Light one candle.

And in you all the families of the earth will be blessed.
— *Genesis 12:3*

OLD PEOPLE HAVING CHILDREN?

Imagine it's Christmas at grandpa and grandma's house. Before everyone opens their presents, your grandparents say they have some very important news to tell everyone. You gather around the tree, and the smell of hot cider and fresh cookies is in the air. You wait patiently for the big announcement. Will there be a big family vacation to Hawaii? What gift could be big enough for everyone to share? You can hardly wait. Your grandparents finally sit down with big smiles on their faces.

Grandpa says, "Everyone, we have good news."

A ripple of excitement follows murmurs around the room. You can't take it anymore. On the edge of your seat, you blurt out, "What is it?"

Grandma takes over and says, "I'm pregnant!"

Would you be shocked? Of course you would!

The oldest woman in modern history to give birth to a child naturally was a British woman named Dawn Brooke, who gave birth to a healthy baby when she was fifty-nine years old. According to one news account, "the pregnancy had been unplanned and had come as a shock to him [Mr. Brooke] and his wife."[1]

If the Brooke baby seems like a miracle, wait until you hear about the birth of Isaac in the Bible!

In the book of Genesis, we meet a lady named Sarai and her husband, Abram. The Bible says, "Sarai was barren; she had no children" (Gen. 11:30). This was despite the fact that Abram's name meant "exalted father." It must have been an embarrassing name to have, but God had a plan for this older couple. When Abram was seventy-five and Sarai was sixty-five, God told them he was going to make them a great nation (Gen. 12:1-3):

> Now the Lord said to Abram,
> "Go forth from your country,
> And from your relatives
> And from your father's house,
> To the land which I will show you;
> And I will make you a great nation,
> And I will bless you,
> And make your name great;
> And so you shall be a blessing;
> And I will bless those who bless you,
> And the one who curses you I
>   will curse.
> And in you all the families of the earth
>   will be blessed."

How would God make them into a great nation and bless all nations of the earth through them if they were too old to have children?

GOD MAKES A COVENANT WITH ABRAM

In Genesis, God takes his promise to bless Abram (and all nations through him) to a whole new level. He makes a covenant with Abram, which is like making a promise. When a covenant was made in the Old Testament, animals were cut in half, their bodies separated to create an open path between the two parts. Then, the two people making the covenant walked that path together to seal the covenant (or promise) between them. In Genesis 15, God makes a covenant with Abram, but instead of both God and Abram walking the path, only God passes between the parts of the sacrificed animal. This meant that God would keep the promise to bless Abram no matter what; the fulfillment of the covenant didn't depend on Abram at all. It completely depended upon God's intervention. But Abram and Sarai are too old to have children. At ninety-nine years old, Abram receives a new name from God. Instead of Abram (which means "exalted father"), his name would be Abraham, which means "father of multitudes." God also changes Sarai's name to Sarah in Genesis 17. When the promise was first made, it seemed to Abram that maybe, just maybe, God could pull it off. Sarai had been sixty-five, but he believed God's word. At the point God gives him a new name, Abraham is ninety-nine and his wife is eighty-nine! Is Abraham just hearing voices, or is God going to deliver?

A DIVINE ANNOUNCEMENT

In Genesis 18, God shows up in human form and has a conversation with Abraham. The personal name of God, Yahweh, is used for the divine visitor. This messenger announces to Abraham that God is going to make good on his promise. He says to Abraham in Genesis 18:10, "'I will surely return to you at this time next year; and behold, Sarah your wife will have a son.' And Sarah was listening at the tent door, which was behind him."

What did Sarah do when she heard God tell Abraham this? Scripture tells us in Genesis 18:12-15:

> Sarah laughed to herself, saying,
> "After I have become old, shall I
> have pleasure, my lord being old
> also?"
> And the LORD said to Abraham, "Why
> did Sarah laugh, saying, 'Shall I
> indeed bear a child, when I
> am so old?' Is anything
> too difficult for the LORD? At
> the appointed time I will return to
> you, at this time next year, and
> Sarah will have a son."
> Sarah denied it however, saying, "I
> did not laugh"; for she was afraid.
> And He said, "No, but you did
> laugh."

A PROMISE COMES TO FRUITION

Can you imagine laughing at something God said? That is exactly what Sarah did. You can imagine the difficulty a ninety-year-old woman would have in believing that she would have a child. It must have sounded crazy! Genesis 21:1-2 tells us, "Then the LORD took note of Sarah as He had said, and the LORD did for Sarah as He had promised. So Sarah conceived and bore a son to Abraham in his old age, at the appointed time of which God had spoken to him."

The promise came true. Abraham was one hundred years old and Sarah was ninety when they had a baby. What a miracle! Christmas is known as the season of miracles because of the birth of Jesus, but long before Jesus came to earth, God brought about this special birth.

QUESTIONS

1. Would you — like Sarah — laugh if you heard that a ninety-year-old woman was going to be pregnant?
2. Why was it funny for Abraham's name to mean "father of multitudes"?
3. Why do you think God waited until Abraham and Sarah were so old before allowing them to have children?
4. What do you need to trust God for today? Do you need a miracle?

PRAYER FOR THE DAY

"God, remind us today that nothing is too difficult for you. We thank you that you are the giver of life and that you performed a miracle with Abraham and Sarah. We thank you that you blessed all the nations of the earth through them."

ISAAC THE SACRIFICE
THE FIRST SPECIAL BIRTH BROUGHT LAUGHTER

December 2nd
Light one candle.

Abraham called the name of his son who was born to him, whom Sarah bore to him, Isaac.

— Genesis 21:3

LAUGHTER

They say laughter is the best medicine. Many doctors over the years have promoted the benefits of hearty laughter. In fact, in 1995, Dr. Madan Kataria started a laughing club. The idea was simple. Several people would meet first thing every morning and form a circle. One person would stand in the middle and tell a joke. The group would break out in exuberant laughter. This lasted for a while until the group ran out of jokes. Later, Dr. Kataria developed a program that helped continue the laughter; the movement resulted in over five thousand Laughter Clubs in forty countries.

You may not know this, but the name Isaac means

"laughter." Abraham and Sarah named their son Isaac because when people heard that someone as old as Sarah had a child, they would laugh (Gen. 21:6)! It's hard to picture a one-hundred-year-old Abraham crawling around on the ground inside the tent playing with Isaac, isn't it? The story of Isaac is a great reminder that God can do incredible things.

We aren't told much about Isaac's childhood, but we do know that parts of it were certainly difficult. Isaac had a half-brother named Ishmael. Ishmael was not the "son of the promise." Ishmael was born from Abraham having sexual relations with a woman named Hagar. Abraham did this (and Sarah allowed it) because the couple didn't believe it was possible for Sarah to have a child. Do you remember what God in human form asked Abraham and Sarah? He asked, "Is anything too difficult for the Lord?" God kept his promise, and according to Hebrews 11:17, Isaac — the "only begotten son" of Abraham and Sarah — was born.

LAUGHTER TURNS TO DIFFICULTY

Genesis 21:9 tells us that Ishmael bullied Isaac by making fun of him. You can imagine that the blessing and miraculous birth of Isaac overshadowed Ishmael a little bit. Ishmael would have known that Isaac was the special son, given the circumstances of his miraculous birth, and Isaac would have known it, too. Isaac must have heard the story of his miraculous birth thousands of times as he grew up. It's likely he felt pressure to be as miraculous and special in life as he was in birth. His very name was a reminder of the covenant and of the miraculous nature of his birth. I can imagine being the son of the promise was not always easy.

As Christians, we are children of promise, too. John 1:12 tells us, "But as many as received Him, to them He gave the right to become children of God, *even* to those who believe in His name." This passage tells us that if we have received Christ, we are his children. We are never told that being a child of God is going to be easy. In fact, Jesus urges us on many occasions to count the cost before signing up to follow him. In the Gospel of Luke, Jesus says, "Whoever does not carry his own cross and come after Me cannot be My disciple. For which one of you, when he wants to build a tower, does not first sit down and calculate the cost to see if he has enough to complete it? Otherwise, when he has laid a foundation and is not able to finish, all who observe it begin to ridicule him, saying, 'This man began to build and was not able to finish'" (Lk. 14:28-30).

Difficulties and trials are a part of the Christian life. We must all count the cost of following Jesus. The blessing for us as believers is that we have an eternal hope in heaven that can never be taken away from us. John 16:33 says, "In the world you have tribulation, but take courage; I have overcome the world." Jesus has conquered death, and in him, we are more than conquerors. Today, no matter how bad your situation may seem, take a step back from it and, like Paul, say, "What then shall we say to these things? If God is for us, who is against us?" (Rom. 8:31). If you have trusted in Christ as your Savior, then take courage because the Bible says you are sealed for the day of redemption! For Isaac, the problems he faced with his brother, Ishmael, were nothing compared to what would happen next.

QUESTIONS

1. What does the name Isaac mean in the Hebrew language?
2. Why would Abraham and Sarah give Isaac such a name?
3. Was it easy for Isaac to live with his older half-brother, Ishmael?
4. Does Jesus promise us that the Christian life will always be easy?

PRAYER FOR THE DAY

"Father, we thank you that we can face difficulty and know that you are still the one in charge. We thank you for the story of Isaac that reminds us that even though he was the son of the promise, life was not always easy. Help us to be faithful in good times and in bad."

ISSAC THE SACRIFICE
THE LORD PROVIDES

December 3rd
Light one candle.

Now it came about after these things, that God tested Abraham,
and said to him, "Abraham!" And he said, "Here I am." He
said, "Take now your son, your only son, whom you love, Isaac,
and go to the land of Moriah, and offer him there as a burnt
offering on one of the mountains of which I will tell you."

— *Genesis 22:1-2*

NO LAUGHING MATTER

What would you be willing to give up for God? Jesus says
in the New Testament that a believer should be ready to
bear a cross for him (Lk. 9:27). Would you die for God?
You might say you would, but an even harder question
might be: could you kill for God? Abraham and Sarah had
waited a long time for their promised child, and now God
wants Abraham to kill Isaac! It seems crazy, doesn't it?

Genesis 22 tells us that "God tested Abraham."
Remember that God's character is not being tested; this is

a test for Abraham. John Sailhamer says that these three words (God tested Abraham) are of utmost importance for the beginning of this story. He says, "Without it God's request that Abraham offer up Isaac as a 'burnt offering' would be inexplicable. By stating clearly at the start that 'God tested Abraham' (v.1), the writer quickly allays any doubt about God's real purpose. There is, then, no thought of an actual sacrifice of Isaac in the narrative, though in the mind of Abraham within the narrative that, of course, was the only thought that was entertained."[1] In other words, the reader is assured that Abraham was fully willing to be obedient to God, yet God never intended for Abraham to kill his child. As far as Abraham knew, this was no test; this was as real as it gets.

The most amazing thing about the story happens next. It doesn't seem that Abraham faces a huge moral dilemma. He doesn't sit around the campfire debating whether he has heard from the Lord. The Scriptures simply record in verse 3: "So, Abraham rose early in the morning and saddled his donkey, and took two of his young men with him and Isaac his son; and he split wood for the burnt offering, and arose and went to the place which God had told him." He didn't try to find a loop hole or a way out of it.

After the miraculous birth of Isaac, I am sure Abraham now believed God could do anything. Think about what Abraham had witnessed. Romans 4:19 says, "Without becoming weak in faith he contemplated his own body, now as good as dead since he was about a hundred years old, and the deadness of Sarah's womb...." When Isaac was conceived, God supernaturally brought Sarah's womb to life. At ninety years old, she was no longer barren!

Abraham had seen a dead womb come to life (Rom. 4:19). Now, in Genesis 22, he expects to see his dead son come back to life (Heb. 11:19). This takes faith to an entirely new level.

As Abraham's testing draws near, Genesis 22:7-9 says, "Isaac spoke to Abraham his father and said, 'My father!' And he said, 'Here I am, my son.' And he said, 'Behold, the fire and the wood, but where is the lamb for the burnt offering?' Abraham said, 'God will provide for Himself the lamb for the burnt offering, my son.'"

The Hebrew word for *provide* is *moriah*. More than a thousand years later, on this mountain where Abraham and Isaac faced this test, Solomon's Temple would be built (2 Chron. 3:1). Lots of lambs would be slaughtered for the sins of the nation on Mount Moriah. Would Isaac be the first? Genesis 22:10 says, "Abraham stretched out his hand and took the knife to slay his son." In that very moment, the Bible tells us that the Lord stopped Abraham. The test was complete. Abraham passed the most difficult examination of faith ever! He was willing to sacrifice his only begotten son. Verse 13 says, "Then Abraham raised his eyes and looked, and behold, behind him a ram caught in the thicket by his horns; and Abraham went and took the ram and offered him up for a burnt offering in the place of his son." God provided!

QUESTIONS

1. Was the testing of Abraham also a test of God's character? What does Sailhamer say about that?

2. What comes to mind when you hear Isaac called Abraham's "only begotten son"?
3. What is so significant about the fact that "Abraham rose early in the morning and saddled his donkey" after receiving the command to sacrifice Isaac?
4. What does *moriah* mean?
5. What comes to mind when you hear this phrase: God will provide for Himself the lamb?
6. How strong is your faith that God will provide for you? What would you be willing to give up for God?

PRAYER FOR THE DAY

"Father, thank you for the example of Abraham's faith. I also thank you today, Lord, that you provided the lamb for him. Help me to trust you for all my needs, no matter what difficulties the day brings."

PART TWO

Jacob the Nation

JACOB THE NATION
HEEL GRABBER

December 4th
Light two candles.

Afterward his brother came forth with his hand holding on to Esau's heel, so his name was called Jacob; and Isaac was sixty years old when she gave birth to them.
— *Genesis 25:26*

THE PROBLEM

Isaac's wife, Rebekah, had the same struggle as that of his mother, Sarah. She was barren. The same Hebrew word *acar* is used for her condition (Gen. 25:21). Infertility can be a horrible struggle for couples. My wife, Amy, and I, Martin, struggled with infertility for several years. My wife had surgery and took fertility medicine to no avail. After we adopted (which was a huge blessing) and had given up hope of a naturally born child, Amy suddenly became pregnant when we least expected it! It truly felt like a miracle. Isaac and Rebekah were certainly relieved when, after twenty years of marriage, Rebekah finally became pregnant! The pain of infertility was removed by the hand of God!

A DIVINE ANNOUNCEMENT

As the story continues, the Bible tells us that Rebekah experienced some kind of struggle within her womb. If you have never seen a baby kick while in a mother's belly, it is quite a thing to behold. Whatever was going on with Rebekah seemed peculiar to her, so she inquired of God. The Lord answered her and said, "Two nations are in your womb; and two peoples will be separated from your body; and one people shall be stronger than the other; and the older shall serve the younger" (Gen. 25:23). He knew all the details of what was coming, just as he knows our futures today.

A PROMISE COMES TO FRUITION

Genesis 25:24-26 says, "When her days to be delivered were fulfilled, behold, there were twins in her womb. Now the first came forth red, all over like a hairy garment; and they named him Esau. Afterward his brother came forth with his hand holding on to Esau's heel, so his name was called Jacob; and Isaac was sixty years old when she gave birth to them."

Jacob's name means "holder of the heel" or "supplanter." A supplanter is someone who overthrows someone else or interferes with their plans.

Jacob and Esau's childhood together was less than cordial at times. In fact, Jacob almost made a game out of trying to cheat Esau out of everything that was valuable to him. Jacob was very ambitious and intelligent. Esau was strong and loved to hunt, but he hated to think. Jacob considered his future while Esau lived in the moment. As God had prophesied to Rebekah, the older (Esau) ended up serving the younger (Jacob).

THE BIRTHRIGHT AND THE BLESSING

The birthright was something typically reserved for the firstborn son. Whoever had the birthright would inherit the father's property and be the head of the household. Deuteronomy 21:17 says that a double portion of the inheritance would go to the firstborn son. However, in the situation of Jacob and Esau, Esau despised his birthright and traded it to Jacob for a bowl of stew! This was a serious mistake on the part of Esau and a calculated move on the part of Jacob (Gen. 25:29-34).

If that wasn't bad enough, Jacob wasn't finished with his brother. When it came time for the family blessing to be passed down from Isaac to Esau, Jacob deceived his brother and his father and stole the blessing. When Esau realized that Jacob had stolen his blessing, "he said, 'Is he not rightly named Jacob, for he has supplanted me these two times? He took away my birthright, and behold, now he has taken away my blessing'" (Gen. 27:36). At this point in the story, Jacob's name fits him pretty well. He has left his family a mess, so much so that Esau actually wants to kill him (Gen. 27:41). This story looks like it is going to repeat the story of Cain and Abel, but some twists are coming. God is going to take hold of Jacob's heel-grabbing heart.

QUESTIONS

1. What problem did Rebekah have that Sarah had before her?
2. How long had Isaac and Rebekah been married before they had the twins? How old was Isaac when they were born?
3. What does Jacob's name mean? Why is it an appropriate name?
4. What was the birthright? What does Esau say that he is going to do to Jacob after Jacob steals the blessing?
5. How did God show that he already knew the future in this story? Do you trust God with your future?
6. From what has happened so far in the story, would you think Jacob has a bright future?

PRAYER FOR THE DAY

"Dear Heavenly Father, I know that I can trust you. I know that the future is already in your hands and that you have a plan for my life. Help me to walk in your plan for my life, and help me to bless others around me."

JACOB THE NATION
A LOVE STORY

December 5th
Light two candles.

When Jacob saw Rachel the daughter of Laban his mother's brother, and the sheep of Laban his mother's brother, Jacob went up and rolled the stone from the mouth of the well and watered the flock of Laban his mother's brother. Then Jacob kissed Rachel and lifted his voice and wept.

— *Genesis 29:10-11*

A PURE BRIDE FOR A PURE NATION

As Jacob was getting ready to flee from his brother Esau, he received some last-minute instructions from his father about where to go. The Bible says in Genesis 28:1-2, "So Isaac called Jacob and blessed him and charged him, and said to him, 'You shall not take a wife from the daughters of Canaan. Arise, go to Paddan-aram, to the house of Bethuel your mother's father; and from there take to yourself a wife from the daughters of Laban your mother's brother.'"

Isaac is basically insisting that Jacob take a wife of pure blood from a specific family instead of marrying an unclean Canaanite. Isaac also blesses Jacob with the covenant that was promised to Abraham and himself. Jacob will now be the one through whom the nations of the Earth will be blessed. Genesis 28:4 says, "May He also give you the blessing of Abraham, to you and to your descendants with you, that you may possess the land of your sojournings, which God gave to Abraham." Wow! First Jacob receives the birthright, then the blessing, and now the covenant promises of Abraham, even though he supplanted his brother and deceived his father. Talk about the undeserved kindness of God!

THE SHOW OFF

Have you ever seen a guy show off to impress a girl? It can be a little embarrassing, can't it?

One day, I (Martin) was walking with my son on the treadmills at the gym. A man waltzed in with headphones on, singing out loud, and chose a treadmill by some pretty young ladies. He was definitely trying to be cool; he raised his voice and kept bringing attention to his muscles. Suddenly, he lost his balance, dumped his water bottle, fell hard, and flew off the end of the treadmill!

Well, things go a little better for Jacob when he decides to show off than they did for the guy at the gym. When Jacob arrives at his destination, he comes to a large watering hole. The Bible is pretty specific about the details concerning the well: "Now the stone on the mouth of the well was large. When all the flocks were gathered there, they would then roll the stone from the mouth of the well and water the sheep, and put the stone back in its place on the mouth of the well" (Genesis 29:2-3). Notice the key words "*they* would then roll the stone from the mouth of the well" (emphasis mine). Apparently, under normal circumstances, it took more than one person to move the stone. Genesis 29:10-11 says, "When Jacob saw Rachel the daughter of Laban his mother's brother, and the sheep of Laban his mother's brother, **Jacob went up and rolled the stone from the mouth of the well** and watered the flock of Laban his mother's brother. Then Jacob kissed Rachel, and lifted his voice and wept" (emphasis mine). What an introduction! Jacob, in a show of strength, moved the stone by himself, watered the sheep, and then kissed Rachel before he said anything to her!

Do you think he may have been coming on a little too strong? Guys have been known to show off for the woman they love. Jacob was no exception. Jacob was also obeying his father's command to seek out a pure wife. Rachel was part of the extended family. This was incredibly important for the Israelites of the future. Israel would later be warned time and time again not to marry Canaanites. Deuteronomy 7:1-4 explains that intermarrying with Canaanites would "turn [the Israelites] from following [God] to serve other gods" which would kindle "the anger of the LORD against [the Israelites]" and prompt God to "quickly destroy" them. Even though Moses and many others would marry foreign wives, as time went on in the Old Testament, the list of banned nations grew from the seven Canaanite nations to encompass all the foreign wives that the Judeans had married during the Babylonian exile. In fact, the Judeans were forced to divorce those wives (Ezra 10:11)!

A TASTE OF HIS OWN MEDICINE

Jacob wanted to marry Rachel so badly that he agreed to work for her father, Laban, for seven years. After Jacob completed the seven years of work, Laban deceitfully gave Jacob Rachel's sister, Leah, instead. Jacob, the supplanter, was supplanted! Laban eventually gave Rachel away to Jacob, but this second marriage cost Jacob seven more years of labor. The love story ends with a twist. In fact, even though both women were Jacob's wives, Genesis 29:31 reveals that Jacob did not love Leah. Laban may have tricked Jacob into marrying the wrong daughter, but he couldn't make Jacob love her.

Leah may have been unloved by Jacob, but not by God. In fact, God would use Leah to be the mother of six of the tribes of the nation of Israel. Leah's sons were: Reuben, Simeon, Levi, Judah, Issachar, and Zebulun.

QUESTIONS

1. When Jacob left home, what instructions did Isaac give his son about picking out a wife?
2. Why do you think Isaac didn't want Jacob to marry outside of their tribe?
3. What do we know about the well that Jacob came upon with the shepherds?
4. How was Jacob kind of a show-off for Rachel?
5. How was the supplanter supplanted?
6. Why do you think Leah was unloved by Jacob? Was she unloved by God?

PRAYER FOR THE DAY

"Lord, we thank you for your love for us, that while we were yet sinners, Christ died for us. We pray that you would help us experience your love on a deeper, more personal level. Thank you for loving us even though we, like Jacob, have been deceivers."

JACOB THE NATION
PENIEL/THE FACE OF GOD

December 6th
Light two candles.

So Jacob named the place Peniel, for he said, "I have seen God face to face, yet my life has been preserved."
— *Genesis 32:30*

JACOB RENAMED ISRAEL

Persistence can be a wonderful gift. Take our sixteenth president, Abraham Lincoln, for instance.

In 1838 he sought to become speaker of the state legislature and was defeated. In 1840, two years later, he sought to become the elector of the state, and was defeated. Three years later he ran for Congress and lost. In 1846 he ran again for Congress and won. Only two years later he ran for reelection and was soundly defeated. In 1849 he sought the job of land officer in his home state but was rejected. In 1854 he ran for the Senate of the United States. Again, he lost. In 1856 he sought the vice-presidential nomination at his party's national convention. He got less than one hundred votes, suffering yet another embarrassing defeat.[1]

Earlier in his career, friends noticed the incredible toll that constant defeat was having on him and worried he might commit suicide. He was so down that he broke off his relationship with a girl he wanted to marry for fear that he couldn't support her financially.[2] Eventually, he struggled through these difficulties and became the president in 1860! Lincoln would become one of the most beloved presidents of all time and the signer of the Emancipation Proclamation that freed the slaves! Paul Tetreault, director of Ford's Theatre where Lincoln was assassinated, claims that more books have been written about Abraham Lincoln in world history than any other except Jesus Christ.[3] Many great men and women have accomplished incredible things because of their persistence in the face of difficulty.

The Bible teaches that Jacob had this kind of persistence. Even before he was born, he wanted to be in first place. He held on to his brother's foot from inside his mother's womb! As a young man, he conspired against his older brother, Esau, to take advantage of him. After he had accomplished his goal of stealing the two most important things that the family offered, he went off and impressed the girl of his dreams (Rachel), wrestled with God, and eventually bore the name of God's people, Israel. Jacob was certainly an ambitious man! After several years of marriage to first Leah, then Rachel, Jacob turned the tables on Laban. Again, Jacob came out on top. Genesis 31:1-3 says, "Now Jacob heard the words of Laban's sons, saying, 'Jacob has taken away all that was our father's, and from what belonged to our father he has made all this wealth.' Jacob saw the attitude of Laban, and behold, it was not friendly toward him as formerly. Then the LORD said to Jacob, 'Return to the land of your fathers and to your relatives, and I will be with you.'"

The only problem with going back home was that Esau was there — and *that* was a *big* problem. Jacob was scared! In fact, he told his servants the night before he was to meet Esau to give Esau several presents to butter him up (Gen. 32:13-21). That night, Jacob was left alone until daybreak. The Bible tells us that Jacob wrestled with a man all night. The wrestling was so intense that Jacob dislocated his hip. Even with an injury, Jacob wouldn't give up and kept holding onto the man. The Scriptures record:

> Then [the man] said, "Let me go, for
> the dawn is breaking."
> But [Jacob] said, "I will not let you go
> unless you bless me."
> So he said to him, "What is your
> name?"
> And he said, "Jacob."
> He said, "Your name shall no longer
> be Jacob, but Israel; for you have
> striven with God and with men
> and have prevailed."
> Then Jacob asked him and said,
> "Please tell me your name."
> But he said, "Why is it that you ask
> my name?" And he blessed him
> there.
> So Jacob named the place Peniel,
> for he said, "I have seen God face
> to face, yet my life has been
> preserved" (Gen. 32:26-30).

The man Jacob wrestled was no man at all. He was wrestling with God in human form! When God shows up in human form, we call it a theophany. At this special moment in history, Jacob saw the face of God and was renamed "Israel." Eventually, the story goes on to tell us that Jacob reconciled with his brother, Esau. The blessing of Abraham began coming to fruition as God preserved Jacob's life. Jacob went on to have twelve sons, and he became the father of the original twelve tribes that inherited the Land of Promise. He was the father of the nation of Israel, which was called after his new name.

PROMISES UNFULFILLED FOR THE NATION

The Hebrew Old Testament has three sections to it: the Law, the Prophets, and the Writings. In all three of these sections, there are special promises that all nations of the earth will be blessed by God. Deuteronomy 32:43 (as part of the Law) promises that the nations will one day be grafted into God's people. In the Prophets, Isaiah 11:10 makes the same claim. Finally, the Writings also include promises for the Gentile nations in Psalm 117:1.

Even though these promises for the nations existed, Israel remained a religion mostly cut off from the rest of the world until the time of Jesus. The nation of Israel under the Old Covenant spread into the Land of Promise but ended up barren — just like the women we've been discussing. And just like the barren mothers who needed divine intervention to give birth, the nation of Israel needed divine intervention in order to graft in the nations. Isaiah 54:1-3 says:

Shout for joy, O barren one, you who have borne no child;
break forth into joyful shouting and cry aloud, you who

have not travailed; for the sons of the desolate one will be more numerous than the sons of the married woman," says the LORD. "Enlarge the place of your tent; stretch out the curtains of your dwellings, spare not; lengthen your cords and strengthen your pegs. For you will spread abroad to the right and to the left. And your descendants will possess nations and will resettle the desolate cities.

This passage clearly looks forward to a future when Israel will no longer be "barren" among the Gentile nations but instead fruitful. These promises of Gentile inclusion only come to fulfillment through the coming of the Messiah, Jesus.

QUESTIONS

1. Name some things about Jacob's personality that demonstrate his persistent attitude.
2. Who was Jacob wrestling with in Genesis 32? What did he want from the visitor?
3. What did the visitor do to Jacob's hip?
4. Did Esau kill Jacob or did Esau receive Jacob?
5. How many sons did Jacob have?
6. Did Old Testament Israel fully include all Gentile nations?
7. Are you persistent when you ask God for things? How is persistence a good characteristic for someone to have?
8. Share some facts that you have learned about Jacob.

PRAYER FOR THE DAY

"Father, help me to be persistent in following you. Help me overcome the difficulty and adversity life throws at me. I thank you for the story of Jacob and Esau. I thank you that the brothers were able to reconcile. Help me to be forgiving, loving, and willing to reconcile with anyone that has done harm to me."

PART THREE

Joseph the Forgiver

JOSEPH THE FORGIVER
THE BELOVED, THE BETRAYED

December 7th
Light three candles.

So it came about, when Joseph reached his brothers, that they stripped Joseph of his tunic, the varicolored tunic that was on him; and they took him and threw him into the pit. Now the pit was empty, without any water in it.

— *Genesis 37:23-24*

THE PROBLEM

Genesis 29:31 tells us that "Rachel was barren." As Rachel dealt with this difficulty, Leah did not struggle at all with her fertility. As it was with Sarah and Rebekah, God would have to open Rachel's womb supernaturally.

Jacob was deceived by Laban, who tricked him into marrying Leah. Now Jacob was married to both sisters, but only Leah was able to give him children. This was a horrible distress to Rachel. Jacob's love was not able to overcome the pain Rachel felt from not being able to bear children. In the ancient world, being unable to bear a child was seen as a curse from God. God not only commanded men and women to "be fruitful and multiply" (Gen. 1:28) but also cursed the wicked with barrenness (Lev. 20:20-21; Jer. 22:30), although we understand today that barrenness was not always the result of a curse.

Rachel had to wonder if her future held only barrenness. Would God intervene?

A DIVINE ANNOUNCEMENT

Genesis 30:22 says, "Then God remembered Rachel, and God gave heed to her and opened her womb." When life is inundated with hardship, we need to remember this verse. *God remembered Rachel.* The power of those three simple words! If you are experiencing a difficult season, know that God has not forgotten you. He has a plan! A similar phrase is used in Exodus 2:24. After four hundred years of slavery to the Egyptians, God's people cried out to him. The Bible says, "So God heard their groaning; and God remembered His covenant with Abraham, Isaac, and Jacob."

God remembered Rachel, he remembered his covenant, and he will remember you!

A PROMISE COMES TO FRUITION

Genesis 30:23-24 says, "So she conceived and bore a son and said, 'God has taken away my reproach.' She named him Joseph, saying, 'May the LORD give me another son.'" Joseph was favored from the time he was young. If this wasn't enough, Jacob — now called Israel — makes Joseph a "varicolored tunic." Some believe the Hebrew here indicates a "full-length robe" or even a "big-sleeved robe." Whatever it was, it was a source of envy and strife between Joseph and his brothers. The Scriptures tell us that Israel made this special tunic himself instead of buying it or having it made. We also know that, in the ancient world, clothes were costly. So then, Joseph received a costly, handcrafted robe from his father, demonstrating clear favoritism. Joseph's brothers hated him and couldn't even speak to him on friendly terms.

In Genesis 37:5-8 and 37:9-11, Joseph makes things worse by telling his brothers of two dreams that suggested he would lead his family and be exalted above them! They must have thought his new robe had caused his head to swell. It would have been absurd to suggest the second-to-youngest son could rule over the elder sons and their parents. The Scriptures record:

> Then Joseph had a dream, and when he told it to his brothers, they hated him even more. He said to them, "Please listen to this dream which I have had; for behold, we were binding sheaves in the field, and lo, my sheaf rose up and also stood erect; and behold, your sheaves gathered around and bowed down to my sheaf."
>
> ... Now he had still another dream, and related it to his brothers, and said, "Lo, I have had still another dream; and behold, the sun and the moon and the eleven stars were bowing down to me" (Gen. 37:5-7, 9).

If his brothers weren't enraged enough by the first dream, Joseph went on to tell them of the second! Clearly, Joseph did not know how to read a room. Even his father rebuked him. But the story didn't end there.

THE WRATH OF HIS BROTHERS

Eventually, Israel sent Joseph to oversee his brothers as they worked in the fields. When his brothers saw the "dreamer" coming, they plotted to kill him. You might be thinking that perhaps he should have kept his dreams to himself. Well, Joseph might have been thinking the same thing when, instead of being welcomed by his brothers, they threw him in a pit. They decided not to kill him, but they didn't know what to do with him yet. You can imagine the anguish Joseph must have felt as he begged his brothers to let him out. They were closest to him, and they betrayed him. Eventually, they sold him to a group of travelling slave traders.

Would God remember Joseph as he had remembered Rachel?

QUESTIONS

1. Why is the statement "God remembered Rachel" so important for each of us to remember?
2. Who was the baby born to Rachel?
3. What are the different kinds of robes that Israel could have fashioned for his son?
4. Talk about Joseph's dreams. Do you think he should have kept them to himself?
5. Do you think God is going to remember Joseph?

PRAYER FOR THE DAY

"Father, thank you for remembering Rachel! I thank you for this story. That you opened the womb of a barren woman yet again is

an amazing testimony of your power. I praise you for the
promises that you made to Joseph and what you did in his life."

JOSEPH THE FORGIVER
NEVER ALONE

December 8th
Light three candles.

The LORD was with Joseph…
— Genesis 39:2

A NEW CHAPTER, ALL ALONE

I (Daniel) will never forget that day — July 1, 1990 — when my parents dropped me off at the United States Military Academy. Nearly sixteen hundred new cadets had assembled with family members in a large basketball arena. A couple of dignitaries spoke, but I don't remember who they were. I was in a daze; my life was about to change radically and not so much for the better. Then, that dreaded moment came as the person in charge said, "New cadets, you have one minute to say goodbye to your loved ones." My heart sank below my belt. I reached over to hug my dad. He was crying. I may have only seen him cry three times in my entire life; this was one of those times. My mom hugged my neck and said, "Go with God." She was smiling but hurting, her face drenched in tears. The shortest minute of my life ended as I broke from the embrace and walked down the steps to the center of the arena. I looked back once. They hadn't moved. With a deep breath, I turned back toward my new chapter with an emptiness and a heaviness I will never forget. I felt completely alone.

BETRAYED AND SOLD INTO SLAVERY

Can you imagine Joseph's thoughts and feelings? I can't. As hard as my experience was in 1990, it pales in comparison to being betrayed by family and sold into slavery. He was forced on a journey from which he undoubtedly thought he would never return. The Bible doesn't give us the details of Joseph's slave-trade experience. Genesis 37:36 ends the chapter by simply stating, "Meanwhile, the Midianites sold him in Egypt to Potiphar, Pharaoh's officer, the captain of the bodyguard." Genesis 39 picks up this historical account by reminding us that Joseph is now in the house of Potiphar. But next comes a surprising statement. Genesis 39:2 says, "The LORD was with Joseph."

One might think that if God was with Joseph, his father would rescue him and bring him home. Or maybe his brothers would have a change of heart, search for Joseph, and find him. However, that is not what happened. God was with Joseph in the pit. God was with Joseph on the trip to Egypt at the hands of the Midianites. God was with Joseph on the slave trade block. And God was with Joseph in the house of his new master.

LIES AND PRISON

Not only was the Lord with Joseph, but the Bible also says that, as a result, "he became a successful man" (Gen. 39:2). Because of God's favor and presence with Joseph, Potiphar quickly promoted him up the ranks to become second-in-command of his entire household. Everything seemed to be going great for Potiphar because of God's favor with Joseph.

But Potiphar's wife found herself very attracted to the young and handsome Joseph. As Potiphar was away, she began to make attempts to seduce Joseph. Yet, Joseph did not succumb to the temptation. Finally, one day, she made a very aggressive advance. Joseph responded, "How can I do such a wicked thing and sin against God?" Since she couldn't have him, she lied about him, falsely accusing him of attacking her. Potiphar, of course, believed his wife and condemned Joseph to prison. So Joseph, once again, suffered tragedy through no fault of his own. He goes to prison. But, once again, we see that shocking phrase, "the LORD was with him." In his toughest moments, Joseph was not alone.

FORGOTTEN IN AN EGYPTIAN PRISON

Once in prison, God's favor continued to be with Joseph. The warden quickly recognized God's favor and put him in charge of all the other prisoners. During this time, on the same night, two inmates had dreams. Joseph noticed their fallen countenances and asked them why they were sad. They told Joseph about their dreams and, in turn, Joseph responded with the meanings of the dreams according to his God-given understanding. One prisoner would be executed and the other — the cup bearer —

would be restored to the service of Pharaoh. Joseph's interpretations came about just as predicted. He requested that the cup bearer remember him, speak well of him to Pharaoh, and get him out of prison. Upon being restored to his position with Pharaoh, however, this cup bearer forgot all about Joseph.

Loneliness can hit us hard at Christmas. Some grieve loved ones lost. Others lament never having loved ones at all. Maybe you aren't able to provide a "good Christmas" for your children or grandchildren. Christmas can be, for many, a depressing time of year. But the good news is this: God is with you. Jesus is called Immanuel which means "God with us." Maybe life is hard right now. Maybe you've been betrayed, sold out, neglected, or even forgotten. Don't despair! Just like God was with Joseph, he is with you!

QUESTIONS

1. What reason did Joseph give for refusing the advances of Potiphar's wife?
2. According to Genesis, why did Joseph do so well under Potiphar and then the prison warden?
3. Do you think you could keep a God-trusting attitude after all Joseph had been through?
4. Have you ever felt the despair that can come from loneliness? How does your church family help fill the void of loneliness?
5. Maybe you are feeling lonely this Christmas. Do you know that Christ has not forgotten you?

PRAYER FOR THE DAY

"Father, I pray you will fill me up today with your presence. Help me to know that you are near. I thank you for the story of Joseph that reminds me that no matter how difficult life becomes, you are with me. I pray that today your Spirit would encourage me and walk with me."

JOSEPH THE FORGIVER
FORGIVING AND SAVING

December 9th
Light three candles.

As for you, you meant evil against me, but God meant it for good in order to bring about this present result, to preserve many people alive.

— *Genesis 50:20*

THE DILEMMA

What do you do if revenge is in your reach? What if you have the authority, the opportunity, and the power to get revenge? How do you process those painful moments and seasons when you are betrayed?

My (Daniel's) grandfather Carl grew up in a wealthy family. His father, Luther, owned a silver mine in eastern Tennessee. In the late 19th century and early 20th century, Luther was doing very well. However, Luther contracted tuberculosis and died rather young. My grandfather was only eleven when Luther died. Carl's mother remarried soon after, and his new stepfather assumed ownership of the mine.

However, Carl's new stepfather already had children of his own. About fifteen years later, both Carl's mother and his stepfather passed away. He expected to inherit his father's mine, company, and wealth since he was the only son of Luther – but that did not happen. His stepfather left all of his wealth to his children and left Carl out completely! From that point forward, Carl felt betrayed by not only his stepfather, but especially his mother. So, instead of living a life of wealth, my grandfather endured the Great Depression of the 1930s with a young family in abject poverty. How does one deal with this kind of betrayal?

THE PHARAOH'S DREAMS

In yesterday's reading, Joseph asked his fellow inmate, the cup bearer, to remember him when he was restored to his position of serving Pharaoh, but the cup bearer forgot. A few years passed and the cup bearer finally remembered Joseph. Pharaoh had some disturbing dreams that no one could interpret. The cup bearer recommended Joseph as an interpreter. Pharaoh sent for Joseph and explained the dreams. God gave Joseph the meaning of the dreams, and he explained God was revealing the future to Pharaoh. There would be seven years of plenty followed by seven years of intense famine. Then Joseph proceeded to advise Pharaoh concerning the best way to prepare. Impressed, Pharaoh exalted Joseph to second-in-command over all of Egypt so Joseph could carry out God's plan to save Egypt — and Joseph's family — from the coming famine.

A POWER CHANGE

As a result, Joseph found himself in a position of power and authority when he encountered his brothers for the first time since they had sold him into slavery. Just as his teenage dreams had predicted, Joseph's brothers came to bow before him and ask him for help. The famine had hit hard in Canaan as well as in Egypt, so Jacob's family needed help. Of course, they did not recognize Joseph.

Genesis 42-50 recounts the interactions between Joseph and his brothers. What would you do? Your brothers hurt you, stripped you of your coat, threw you in a pit, and sold you into slavery! Now they are standing before you, not knowing who you are, and asking for help. The power of life and death was in Joseph's hands in this moment. But the Lord was with Joseph.

He put his brothers through a series of tests to see where their hearts were. Did they regret what they had done to Joseph? How was Jacob doing, and how did he handle the news of Joseph's plight? Had his brothers repented of their actions? Joseph wanted answers, and he had the power and authority to get them.

GOD PLANNED IT FOR GOOD

In Genesis 45, Joseph revealed himself to his brothers. They were terrified. Yet Joseph's perspective was not one of vengeance but of faith. He said, "Now, therefore, it was not you who sent me here, but God" (v. 8). Joseph then moved his entire family to Egypt so he could care for them — including his father, Jacob. All seemed well for the brothers until Jacob died. Joseph's brothers were concerned that he would exact his revenge once their father was gone. But Joseph says in Genesis 50:19-21 (CSB), "Don't be afraid. Am I in the place of God? You planned evil against me; God planned it for good to bring about the present result — the survival of many people. Therefore, don't be afraid. I will take care of you and your children."

My grandfather carried a heavy bitterness with him his entire life. To my knowledge, he never forgave his mother or his stepfather. Forgiveness is always our choice to make. God, through Christ, forgives a great many of our sins. Now, especially at Christmas, is the time to choose to forgive. Take a cue from Joseph. Trust in the Lord and his plan, and forgive those who've wronged you.

QUESTIONS

1. Do you find it difficult to forgive those who have done you wrong in the past?
2. How bad do you think the pain must have been for Joseph when he saw his brothers in Egypt?
3. What would you have done had you been Joseph in this situation?
4. Are there people from your past you need to forgive? Are there grudges you are still holding that you need to let go? Now is the time to do that. Have the conversations, and make the phone calls, if necessary.
5. Read Romans 8:28. How would this passage apply to Joseph's life?

PRAYER FOR THE DAY

"Lord, help me forgive others. I ask you for a heart like Joseph's. Help me look with pity upon those who have done me harm and remember my own faults and weaknesses. I pray for the strength to always trust that you have my best interests in mind and that you work all things together for good."

PART FOUR

Samson the Savior

SAMSON THE SAVIOR
SUNNY POWER

December 10th
Light four candles.

For behold, you shall conceive and give birth to a son, and no razor shall come upon his head, for the boy shall be a Nazirite to God from the womb; and he shall begin to deliver Israel from the hands of the Philistines.

— *Judges 13:5*

THE PROBLEM

Who had a miraculous birth and was prophesied in the book of Judges to be the savior of Israel (Judg. 13:1-5)? Who would stand in powerful judgment over Israel (15:15)? Who appeared before his interrogators three times (16:6-20) and was betrayed by the most intimate of friends for a certain price of silver (16:5)? Who was bound, mocked, beaten, and dishonored before men (16:21-25)? Who gave up his life to deliver his people with his arms outstretched (16:29-30)? In his death, who provided a much greater deliverance than he ever did during his life

(16:30)? Nobody took this man's life; he laid it down (16:30). Who was he? If you said Jesus, you would be right, but I am actually speaking of Samson!

When we meet the parents of Samson, it is during a tumultuous time in Israelite history referred to as the period of the Judges. Israelite idolatry had led to a cycle wherein God allowed foreign domination over Israel until God raised up a judge to deliver the people and lead them in repentance. Judges 13:2 says, "There was a certain man of Zorah, of the family of the Danites, whose name was Manoah; and his wife was barren and had borne no *children*." As with the previous passages we've discussed, this passage sets the stage for God to do another miraculous work in the midst of barrenness.

A DIVINE ANNOUNCEMENT

"Then the angel of the LORD appeared to the woman and said to her, 'Behold now, you are barren and have borne no *children*, but you shall conceive and give birth to a son'" (Judg. 13:3). This child, however, was to be raised in a special way. The angel goes on to say in verses 4-5, "Now therefore, be careful not to drink wine or strong drink, nor eat any unclean thing. For behold, you shall conceive and give birth to a son, and no razor shall come upon his head, for the boy shall be a Nazirite to God from the womb; and he shall begin to deliver Israel from the hands of the Philistines." This special child was to be set apart for the purpose of serving the living God. This Nazirite vow would have made him unique among his peers. It then becomes clear that this messenger of God was God himself. After making an offering to the Lord, the "angel" (also could be translated *messenger*) disappeared (Judg. 13:20). Manoah and his wife were startled. Realizing that this was God himself, Manoah said, "We shall surely die, for we have seen God." God had spoken the prophecy; a child would be born to Manoah and his wife. It was a sure thing! And sure enough, we see in Judges 13:24 that "the woman gave birth to a son and named him Samson; and the child grew up and the LORD blessed him."

SAMSON WAS SUN-LIKE

Our sun is ninety-three million miles from the earth. Did you know that it is actually a star? It's amazing that we can get a sun burn from ninety-three million miles away! If you're wondering how, it's because the surface of the sun is ten thousand degrees Fahrenheit! It is so powerful that the sunlight that falls on the state of Texas at noon is 301 times the output of all the power plants in the world![1] That kind of power is incredible, isn't it?

The Old Testament contains many stories of Samson's legendary strength. Countless storybooks, sermons, and anecdotes reference Samson, so there's a good chance you've heard his story. But, did you know that Samson's name means "sunny" or "sun-like?"[2] That's right. His name is derived from the Hebrew word for the sun. Like the strength of the sun in the morning, Samson comes bursting into a very dark time in Israelite history. Samson's great strength had many positives, but it also had some big drawbacks. It becomes apparent in Judges 13-16 that he had no fear. Unfortunately, his fearlessness extended to the Lord; he did not fear the Lord or respect the Lord's mandates. He married a Philistine who worshiped false gods. He touched a dead animal, and because of his cavalier, immoral lifestyle, his hair was cut. Both touching something dead and cutting one's hair were strictly prohibited by his lifelong Nazirite vow. He also had a history of sexual immorality with prostitutes (Judg. 16:1).

Sometimes a person's greatest strength can also be their greatest weakness.

QUESTIONS

1. Name three things that quickly come to mind about Samson's life that remind of you of Jesus.
2. How was Samson's greatest strength also his greatest weakness?
3. Why is the name "Sunny" a good name for Samson?
4. What was the name of Samson's lifelong vow?
5. Why do you think Samson didn't fear the Lord like he should have?
6. Proverbs 1:7 says, "The fear of the Lord is the beginning of knowledge; fools despise wisdom and instruction." Talk through this verse in light of Samson's life and yours.

PRAYER FOR THE DAY

"Father, I thank you for the story of Samson. I thank you that you raised up a man that would help relieve Israel from foreign enemies. I pray you would help me see that my greatest strengths can also be my greatest weaknesses. Help me to never swell with pride but instead thank you in humility for your goodness to me."

SAMSON THE SAVIOR
STRENGTHS BECOME WEAKNESSES

December 11th
Light four candles.

He found a fresh jawbone of a donkey, so he reached out and took it and killed a thousand men with it.
— *Judges 15:15*

UNIQUE AMONG THE JUDGES

Samson is clearly different from the judges before and after him. He was charismatic, smart, and physically tough as nails. He must have been an intimidating figure. We are never told he was tall like Goliath, but like the giant who faced David, Samson certainly struck fear into the hearts of men.

Judges 13-16 recounts some of the more famous stories about Samson. I want to look at these stories today a little differently than you may have encountered them in the past. Our tendency is to glorify these stories as demonstrations of the strength of a man. While these stories definitely indicate that Samson had great physical strength, they also illustrate that he had greater moral weaknesses. Samson reminds us that when our gifts aren't used for good, they can quickly lead to evil. These stories do not demonstrate Samson's strength. Instead, they reveal his weaknesses.

THE LION (BROKEN VOWS)

I (Martin) remember hearing the story about Samson killing a lion with his bare hands when I was just a small child in Vacation Bible School. I remember wondering how that could be possible. A few years ago, I read a story about an African herdsman who killed a lion in a similar fashion. "Moses Lekalau, 35, a herdsman, was walking from a neighboring village in Maralal with his livestock when a lion pounced upon him. He managed to fend off the animal and used his bare hands and a spear to kill him following [an] half hour duel."[1] A simple Google search will reveal that Mr. Lekalau is only one of several African herdsmen who have recently killed leopards or lions with their bare hands.

Samson didn't do anything wrong by killing the lion. In fact, he didn't initiate trouble with the lion. He was most likely caught off guard. Judges 14 tells us that Samson wanted to marry a woman who belonged to an idol-worshipping nation. As he was on his way to talk to her with his parents in tow, the Scriptures say, they "came as far as the vineyards of Timnah; and behold, a young lion came roaring toward him. The Spirit of the LORD came upon him mightily, so that he tore him as one tears a young goat..." (v. 5). What crazy strength!

If that was the end of the story, we would be disappointed that he pursued an unbeliever, but we would be left in awe of his strength. However, a few days later,

Samson passed by the dead lion. Honeybees had made their home inside the carcass. Instead of adhering to his Nazirite vow (Judg. 13:4), he scooped up some honey from inside the dead animal. His Nazirite vow forbade him from coming into physical contact with anything dead (Num. 6:6-8).

So, instead of being in awe of his strength, we are left with disappointment in Samson's character.

THIRTY INNOCENT MEN (A MURDERING THIEF)

During the wedding feast, Samson challenged the Philistine men to solve a riddle. If they solved it within the seven days of the feast, they would receive thirty linen garments and thirty changes of clothes. If they couldn't solve it, they would owe the same to Samson. This riddle that Samson was confident the Philistines couldn't solve was about his sin involving the lion. He asked them to solve the following: "Out of the eater came something to eat, and out of the strong came something sweet" (Judg. 14:14). Of course, the Philistines couldn't solve it at first. Eventually, they pressured Samson's new wife, who finally told them the answer. The Philistines answered, "What is sweeter than honey? What is stronger than a lion?" Samson figured out that his new wife had told them. Angry, he rushed to another Philistine city called Ashkelon and murdered thirty men, stealing their clothes to pay the debt of the riddle. Unlike other judges before Samson, whose violence was a response to the slavery, oppression, and attacks from neighboring tribes, Samson attacked the Philistines without real cause. He murdered and stole in a spirit of anger for the sake of his own pride.

THE FOX TAILS

After some days had passed, Samson went back to his wife's home to pick her up. When Samson arrived, he discovered the father of the bride had thought that Samson hated his daughter after the riddle incident. Because of this, the father gave his daughter's hand in marriage to a Philistine man! This enraged Samson who then said, "This time I shall be blameless in regard to the Philistines when I do them harm" (Judg. 15:3). Samson caught three hundred foxes (maybe jackals), tied pairs together by their tails, and set fire to their tails. He then turned them loose into Philistine fields. It utterly ruined their stacked and standing grain piles as well as their olive orchards. Samson, whose name means "sunny," acted with a dark, angry, and vengeful heart.

THE JAWBONE OF A DONKEY

Immediately following this event, the Philistines killed Samson's wife and father-in-law. Samson then hid in the cleft of a rock called Etam. The Philistines demanded the Israelites give Samson over to them. Because Philistia ruled Israel at this time, the Israelites complied. But then Samson proceeded to kill one thousand Philistine men with the jawbone of a donkey.

All of this destruction and death can be traced back to Samson's seemingly simple decision to marry a woman he shouldn't have married. Some may argue that the Spirit of the Lord enabled Samson to do all of this. While it is true that Samson had an extra measure of God's grace and Spirit in his life, he squandered this gift and eventually the Lord left him (Judg. 16:20).

QUESTIONS

1. The powerful acts of Samson are typically celebrated. What might be another way to think of his actions?
2. Do you struggle with broken vows, anger, pride, or revenge? Where will you end up if you continue to live this way?
3. One sin led to another in Samson's life. Where did it all begin?
4. How can you guard against your strengths becoming your weaknesses?

PRAYER FOR THE DAY

"Lord, please forgive me for breaking your law. Help me look at the story of Samson and learn from his mistakes. Help me remain humble and kind, and help me refrain from seeking revenge against those who would seek to do me harm."

SAMSON THE SAVIOR
THE WRONG SACRIFICE

December 12th
Light four candles.

And Samson said, "Let me die with the Philistines!" And he
bent with all his might so that the house fell on the lords and all
the people who were in it. So the dead whom he killed at his
death were more than those whom he killed in his life.

— *Judges 16:30*

SACRIFICE

Sacrifice is great, but only if it is done out of love.

Has anyone ever sacrificed for you, and that sacrifice
made a huge impact on your life? Many have sacrificed for
my (Martin's) family through the years. Once, years ago, a
man and his wife wrote a very kind note to my wife and
me. The note said that they really appreciated all the hard
work our family had put into ministry. The couple also
said they wanted to bless us for working hard, and they
had enclosed a check for our family. When my wife
showed it to me, there were tears in her eyes. It was for

$10,000! Their sacrifice was out of love for my family. It was the right kind of sacrifice, and the effects of it still exist in my life today.

There is also a wrong kind of sacrifice. The apostle Paul tells us in 1 Corinthians 13:3, "… if I give all my possessions to feed the poor, and if I surrender my body to be burned, but do not have love, it profits me nothing." Sacrifice, when connected to love for others, is a beautiful picture of the gospel! But sacrifice can also be used for selfish means such as manipulation or as a way to receive recognition. Imagine if that couple had sent that check to my wife and me but also asked us to do something in my ministry as a favor to them that I would not do otherwise. Then, the sacrifice would not truly have been a gift.

So then, sacrifice can be used for good or for evil. In some cases, as in our story, sacrifice can even be used as a form of revenge.

DELILAH (SAMSON'S DOWNFALL)

Samson continued to spiral downward after the incident with the jawbone. He was intimate with a prostitute (Judg. 16:1) and ran into more trouble by falling in love with a woman named Delilah. The Philistines offered to pay Delilah in silver if she could find out from Samson where his amazing strength came from. He lied to Delilah three different times about how he could be weakened, and each time after she implemented those plots, Philistines charged in to capture him. Samson escaped their grasp each time, but Delilah eventually wore Samson down. He gave up the source of his strength. Samson said, "A razor has never come on my head, for I have been a Nazirite to God from my mother's womb. If I am shaved, then my strength will leave me and I will become weak and be like any other man" (Judg. 16:17). Delilah waited until Samson fell asleep and had his hair shaved off as he slept on her lap. The saddest part comes when he wakes up. As the Philistines begin to attack him, Judges 16:20 records, "And he awoke from his sleep and said, 'I will go out as at other times and shake myself free.' But he did not know that **the LORD had left him**" (emphasis mine).

REVENGE

It is unfortunate that we only see Samson crying out to God when he wants something for himself. The first time was when he became thirsty after killing one thousand Philistines (Judg. 15:18), and the second time was when he asked God to help him avenge himself (Judg. 16:28). The first time Samson asked for help, God answered by splitting the ground so that a fresh spring came out of it. The second time he asked God to help him was when he stretched out his hands and pushed down the pillars of the Philistine temple. We assume God must have intervened because Samson's strength returned long enough for him to succeed, but we are not told that God answered him as we were told the first time. What we do know is that God had left him after his head was shaved and that, after his hair grew back, he was able to push down the pillars of the temple and avenge himself. Scripture does not *say* God specifically, miraculously helped him.

We will contrast Israel's two saviors (Samson and Jesus) in their final moments. But for now, let this verse stick in your head, "Then Samson called to the LORD and said, 'O Lord God, please remember me and please strengthen me just this time, O God, that I may at once be avenged of the Philistines for my two eyes'" (Judg. 16:28).

QUESTIONS

1. Has anyone ever sacrificed for you, and it left a huge impression on your life? Share it with your family.
2. What was wrong with Samson's sacrifice? How does it compare to Christ's?
3. When you sacrifice for others, do you look for recognition?
4. Do you struggle with wanting revenge against those who have wronged you? Do you need to confess and repent of that sin?
5. Samson struggled with selfishness. Are you tempted to be selfish about anything in your life?
6. Can you name all the barren women and children born to them up to his point? Don't cheat; I am asking if you can recall them from memory!

PRAYER FOR THE DAY

"Lord, I pray this story would remind me about my own weaknesses. I pray you would help me live unselfishly. I thank you for the sacrifice of Jesus that sought redemption and not revenge. I pray that today your truth would penetrate my heart."

PART FIVE

Samuel the High Priest

SAMUEL THE HIGH PRIEST
THE LORD HEARD

December 13th
Light five candles.

It came about in due time, after Hannah had conceived, that she gave birth to a son; and she named him Samuel, saying, "Because I have asked him of the Lord."

— 1 Samuel 1:20

THE ONGOING STRUGGLE

Growing up, I (Daniel) had a friend named D.J. whose legs had not quite developed correctly. He was told he would never walk or run like a normal boy and that he would never be able to play sports. Both our dads coached little league football, and both our families were very passionate about the sport. Although D.J. had to wear braces much akin to Forrest Gump, he went to every practice with his dad. He would serve as water boy and towel boy, and he would complete all kinds of tasks just to be around the game. He constantly faced the reality that his dream was made impossible by his handicap.

A young wife named Hannah faced a similar predicament; she watched others living her dream every day, and all the while, she was acutely aware of her own inability. She was married to Elkanah, who was a noble and just man and a good husband, and she longed to provide him with children. Elkanah's other wife, Peninnah, had given Elkanah several children. Hannah yearned to have a child, yet day in and day out Peninnah would remind Hannah of her inability, her *acar*.

HER DESPERATE PLEA

In her desperation, Hannah went to the house of the Lord. The Bible records that Hannah was "deeply distressed" and "prayed to the LORD and wept bitterly" (1 Sam. 1:10). Hannah pleaded with the Lord to not forget her but to remember her and give her a son. She prayed a prayer of dedication, promising that if the Lord would grant her a son, she would give that son to the service of the Lord. So desperate was Hannah in her prayer that the priest Eli, who was observing Hannah, believed she was drunk. Hannah explained her desperation to Eli, who asked the Lord's favor to be upon her.

THE LORD HEARD

The next morning, Elkanah and Hannah worshiped the Lord and returned home. At this point, she had no idea whether the Lord was going to honor her request, yet she worshiped him anyway. In the same verse (1 Sam. 1:19), the author reveals that the Lord remembered Hannah, and she conceived.

DEDICATED

Hannah gave birth to Samuel and, after weening him, took her son to the tabernacle. She approached Eli and said, "I am the woman who stood here beside you, praying to the LORD. For this boy I prayed, and the LORD has given me my petition which I asked of Him. So I have also dedicated him to the LORD; as long as he lives he is dedicated to the LORD" (1 Sam. 1:26-28). And just as his mother promised, Samuel did serve the Lord the rest of his life.

HANNAH'S SONG

Upon giving Samuel to the Lord, she prayed a prayer now recorded in 1 Samuel 2:1-10. Her prayer is filled with rejoicing and praising the Lord for his power, might, and favor. She went to the Lord, who always hears the cries of his people.

MIRACLES HAPPEN

My friend D.J. took a cue from Hannah. He grew up in a devoutly Christian home. His family and church prayed for D.J. often. However, as his struggle continued, he became more and more desperate and took that desperation to the Lord.

The Lord heard D.J.'s cries just as he heard Hannah's so long ago. D.J. was miraculously healed. By the time we were eleven, we played together on a local football team. In fact, D.J. went on to get a full scholarship at Austin Peay State University in Clarksville, Tennessee, to play football.

The Lord hears us. All through Scripture, when God's people cried out to him, he listened. Are you desperate this Christmas? Are you deeply hurting like Hannah? Cry out to the Lord. He will hear you.

QUESTIONS

1. Have you ever pled with God over a trial in your life? What was the outcome? Good or bad, can you look back and see how God may have used it in your larger story?
2. What did Eli think of Hannah when he saw her praying in the tabernacle?
3. How did God "hear Hannah"?
4. What happened to my friend D.J.? Isn't that amazing?

PRAYER FOR THE DAY

"Father, I thank you for hearing every prayer! Help me have faith like Hannah. I thank you for stories like D.J.'s that encourage my faith, and I pray you will do similar things in my life for your glory."

SAMUEL THE HIGH PRIEST
CALLED

December 14th
Light five candles.

And Eli said to Samuel, "Go lie down, and it shall be if He calls you, that you shall say, 'Speak, LORD, for Your servant is listening.'" So Samuel went and lay down in his place.
– 1 Samuel 3:9

THE PROPHECY TO ELI

One day, a "man of God" came to Eli and announced on behalf of God, "But I will raise up for Myself a faithful priest who will do according to what is in My heart and in My soul; and I will build him an enduring house, and he will walk before My anointed always" (1 Sam. 2:35).

The calling starts with God, not us. He initiates this beautiful relationship.

DISCERNING GOD'S VOICE

1 Samuel 3 picks up with a young Samuel serving the Lord by serving in Eli's house. Though Samuel did not know his life's calling, he still faithfully served the Lord in his current situation. What a great truth we learn from Samuel: it is best to serve faithfully in our current situation until God calls us to do something different.

One night as Samuel slept, God called out to him. Samuel ran to Eli and said, "Here I am, for you called me" (v. 5). Eli, awakened suddenly by Samuel's intrusion into his room, replied, "I did not call, lie down again" (v. 5). So Samuel went back to bed. Then, God called out to Samuel a second time. He ran to Eli again and said, "Here I am, for you called me" (v. 6). Again, Eli responded, "I didn't call, my son, lie down again" (v. 6). For the third time, God called Samuel, and for the third time Samuel ran to Eli and said, "Here I am, for you called me" (v. 8). This time Eli understood what was happening. So, he gave Samuel instructions on how to respond. Samuel went back to bed, and God called to him a fourth time. This time, Samuel responded, "Speak, for Your servant is listening" (v. 10). Samuel now knew the voice of the Lord.

A TOUGH MESSAGE

We often hear this historical account and are simply encouraged that a young boy was able to hear from God. However, if we read on, we see that God's voice is instantly met with the challenge to obey. The first message God had for Samuel was not a pleasant one. In fact, we see that Samuel is greatly afraid of delivering God's message to Eli, whose sons had strayed from God. Acting as priests, they had defiled the sanctuary in the tabernacle, and Eli had done nothing to stop them or discipline them in any way. So, the Lord was going to remove Eli's family from the priesthood forever. When morning came, Eli asked Samuel about God's message to the boy. In spite of his fear, Samuel obeyed God and delivered the message. Since he did not allow his fear to cripple him and faithfully obeyed God with this tough message, God showed Samuel favor. Eli accepted God's judgment faithfully, and God continued to show his favor on Samuel (1 Sam. 3:19).

When the Lord speaks to someone in Scripture, a challenge to obey often ensues. But don't be afraid. Obedience to God is always the wise choice. Trust in the Lord just as Eli did when he said, "It is the LORD; let Him do what seems good to Him" (1 Sam. 3:18). When God speaks to you through his Word, obey him, and the favor of the Lord will be upon you.

QUESTIONS

1. Have you ever woken in the middle of the night with the keen sense that God has given you a message? If so, what was that like?
2. What is the difference between Samuel and the sons of Eli?
3. What is the message God gave Samuel?
4. Could you have told Eli the bad news? How hard must that have been for Samuel?

PRAYER FOR THE DAY

"Lord, thank you for these truths today. Thank you for the reminder that you are not only a God of kindness but also of

judgment. I pray you would help me to be as faithful today as Samuel was. Also help me to tell the truth no matter what happens."

SAMUEL THE HIGH PRIEST
THE ONE WHO ANOINTS

December 15th
Light five candles.

Samuel said, "Has the LORD as much delight in burnt offerings and sacrifices as in obeying the voice of the LORD? Behold, to obey is better than sacrifice, and to heed than the fat of rams."
– I Samuel 15:22

GOD VERSUS THE PEOPLE

As a parent, I (Daniel) often deal with ingratitude. Most of the time, my seven children voice their thanks when they should, but there are times when their sinful nature rears its ugly head in the form of entitlement and ingratitude. As a father, I find myself tempted in these times to feel unappreciated and frustrated. God did so much for the Israelites over the centuries through Moses, Joshua, and the judges only to be rejected by his own people over and over. I can't imagine maintaining patience or even consistent, loving discipline through all that, but God did!

The period of the judges is brought to a close when

Israel requested a king. Having the one and only God of the universe as their ruler was not enough for them. They wanted to be like all the other nations. They wanted a human king. Samuel warned them of the perils of having a human king who would take sons and daughters from Israelite families for his service. A human king would seize land and livestock. He would seize one tenth (at least) of all produce from crops. Essentially, the king would take whatever he wanted from whomever he wanted. But Israel did not listen. They were bound and determined; they wanted a king. Samuel rebuked their sin, but he brought their request before God. The Lord told Samuel, "Listen to the voice of the people in regard to all that they say to you, for they have not rejected you, but they have rejected Me from being king over them" (1 Sam. 8:7).

MAN'S CHOICE

God determined to give Israel exactly what they wanted. 1 Samuel 9 introduces us to Saul. Samuel describes Saul as "an impressive young man. There was no one more impressive among the Israelites than he. He stood a head taller than anyone else" (1 Sam. 9:2 CSB). Saul was exactly what Israel thought they wanted in a king. As the Lord directed, Samuel the prophet anointed Saul as king.

Saul's reign quickly took a turn for the worse. Rather than seek the Lord as the Lord had commanded, Saul took it upon himself to offer sacrifices, which was a task reserved for Samuel. His disobedience, lack of patience, and lack of trust in the Lord cost him dearly. Samuel declared to King Saul that his kingdom would not last but that God would appoint another man as ruler over his people (1 Sam. 13:14).

GOD'S CHOICE

The man God appointed was none other than David. Unlike the tall and handsome Saul, David was the runt of his family. In fact, 1 Samuel 16 records how Samuel went to the house of Jesse to anoint one of his sons as the next king. Jesse presented seven sons to Samuel. The Lord rejected all seven of them and told Samuel, "God sees not as man sees, for man looks at the outward appearance, but the LORD looks at the heart" (1 Sam. 16:7). One can only imagine the tone and utter disbelief as Jesse then muttered, "There remains yet the youngest" (v. 11). As young David approached, the Lord said to Samuel, "Arise, anoint him; for this is he" (v. 12). So Samuel anointed David as the next king.

Scripture often reminds us that God's choices are vastly different from ours. God desires the glory, so he chooses the least likely candidates to serve him. When asking how God can use you, don't base your answer on your abilities and expertise but rather on God's ability. He can take your willingness to serve and use you to accomplish things you can't even imagine.

SAMUEL'S LIFE

Hannah's troubled, distraught, and barren beginning begot a man who anointed kings. Samuel lived a faithful life, just as God had foretold. He anointed David, who would receive a special promise from God. Through David's line would come the Messiah. Jesus was born in the City of David (Bethlehem) of the house and lineage of David. How the Lord answered Hannah's prayer!

If you're discouraged this Christmas season, find true hope in the Lord. Our imaginations can't scratch the surface of what God can do in and through your life. Take your desperations to him, and trust in him, his timing, his plan, and his glory.

QUESTIONS

1. What is ingratitude? Do you ever feel that way toward your situation? When they were ungrateful for their true King (Yahweh), the children of Israel were warned about the perils of having an earthly king. Why do you think Israel wanted an earthly king, anyway?
2. What is the difference between how man chooses a king and how God chooses a king? When you look at leaders, do you look at the heart (like God) or the stature of a man (like man)?
3. Who would be anointed after Saul as the king of Israel?

PRAYER FOR THE DAY

"Lord, help me keep you as the true king of my life. Help me look at others the way you look at them. I pray I would not be distracted by what is on the outside but instead look to the heart of a person."

PART SIX

John the Baptist

JOHN THE BAPTIST
THE ELIJAH

December 16th
Light six candles.

Behold, I am going to send you Elijah the prophet before the
coming of the great and terrible day of the LORD. He will restore
the hearts of the fathers to their children and the hearts of the
children to their fathers, so that I will not come and smite the
land with a curse.

– Malachi 4:5-6

THE END OF THE OLD TESTAMENT

If you go to the very last book in the Old Testament,
Malachi, and to the very last verses (Mal. 4:5-6), you will
read about the prophecy of the return of Elijah before the
Day of the Lord. This passage created an expectation in
ancient Israel that Elijah would return prior to the coming
of the Messiah. As God orchestrated his story, the last
event to occur in the Old Covenant timeline was the
coming of John the Baptist. If the coming of Christ is the

inauguration of the New Covenant, then his predecessor, John, is the denouement of the Old Covenant.

A CONVERSATION ABOUT ELIJAH

Matthew 17 records the amazing moment when Jesus was transfigured. Peter, James, and John (the disciple, not the baptist) witnessed this moment. They also saw Moses and Elijah. After this incredible event, Jesus walked down the mountain with his three disciples. With this vision of Elijah fresh on their minds, they asked Jesus about the prophecy of Elijah coming first. Jesus says in Matthew 17:11-12, "Elijah is coming and will restore all things; but I say to you that Elijah already came, and they did not recognize him, but did to him whatever they wished...." The disciples understood Jesus was talking about John the Baptist.

FULFILLED PROPHECY

In addition to fulfilling the prophecy of Malachi, John the Baptist also fulfilled Isaiah 40:3. Matthew 3:3 quotes the prophecy in Isaiah when referencing John the Baptist: "The voice of one crying in the wilderness, 'Make ready the way of the Lord, make His paths straight!'"

Finally, in Mark 1:2, Mark connects John the Baptist to the prophecy of Malachi 3:1 which states, "I am going to send My messenger, and he will clear the way before Me." All these prophecies point to John the Baptist, the one who would prepare the way for the Messiah.

INTERESTING BOOK ENDS

One cannot help but notice the interesting similarities between the first significant birth of the Old Covenant era we discussed and the last significant birth we will discuss from that era. Both Sarah and Elizabeth (John the Baptist's mother) were well advanced in years when they received the promise of a child, meaning they were both biologically unable to conceive children. Just as Sarah had laughed when she heard the news she would give birth to a son in her old age, Elizabeth's husband (Zechariah) did not believe at first, either; thus the Lord struck him mute until the birth of John. Both Sarah and Elizabeth had been barren prior to their supernatural conception. Both wondered how the Lord would achieve such a conception. One gave birth to the man who began the fulfillment of the covenant between God and Abraham, and the other gave birth to the one who would prepare the way for the Messiah and the New Covenant.

QUESTIONS

1. How is John the Baptist's story similar to Isaac's?
2. How is John the Baptist the end of the Old Covenant era?
3. Read the verse under this day's heading (Mal. 4:5-6) and then read Luke 1:17. Do you see a connection?
4. Was John himself the way, or was he only preparing the way?

PRAYER FOR THE DAY

"Father, I thank you for the ministry of John the Baptist. Thank you for fulfilling prophecy by sending him to prepare the way of the Lord. I pray you would help me to be faithful in preparing to

share the gospel with those around me. Help me speak the truth of the gospel to my neighbor and the nations."

JOHN THE BAPTIST
NO ONE GREATER

December 17th
Light six candles.

Truly I say to you, among those born of women there has not arisen anyone greater than John the Baptist!
— *Matthew 11:11*

FAMILIAR COUSINS

I (Daniel) have spent a great deal of time researching my own genealogy. My findings are so fascinating. I have discovered that I am related to Revolutionary and Civil War soldiers. I have found witches and criminals in my past. But I also found that I am related to President Rutherford B. Hayes. In the few times I have engaged in genealogical conversations with someone, who do you think I mention first as one of my distant relatives? President Rutherford B. Hayes.

The Gospels record that Mary (the mother of Jesus) and Elizabeth (the mother of John the Baptist) were relatives. In fact, Luke records that Mary visited Elizabeth while they were both pregnant. Upon meeting, the unborn John the Baptist leapt within his mother's womb at the presence of Jesus, and Elizabeth was filled with the Holy Spirit.

There is little doubt that Elizabeth told this story and others to her son as she raised him. Although John the Baptist might not have met Jesus prior to Jesus's baptism, John must have heard stories about Mary giving birth to the Messiah and how the angel had appeared to both Mary and Joseph, just as he had appeared to Zechariah, John's father. We don't know when John recognized his own role in the unfolding plan of God, but he must have been aware of Mary's son and Jesus's identity as the Messiah.

SURPRISED BY DOUBT

John was in a tough spot due to recent events. He had faithfully proclaimed God's truth, preparing the way for Jesus. He had boldly called out people for their sin and called them to repentance, and he had amassed quite a following. One day, he rebuked the local ruler, Herod the Tetrarch, because Herod was with Herodias, his brother's wife. Herod was humiliated and loathed John the Baptist; he arrested John and put him in prison.

While in prison, John heard about Jesus and some things Jesus was doing. The book of Matthew records something unusual that happened next. John sent his followers to ask Jesus, "Are you the one who is to come, or should we expect someone else?" (Matt. 11:3 CSB). In other words, John the Baptist was having serious doubts about if Jesus was really the Messiah. Had Jesus not done enough? Of course he had; Jesus had proven himself. This issue lay not with Jesus but with John, who was suffering. He was in prison. His life was in danger. He very well could have been experiencing a short crisis of faith. Perhaps sitting in a cell, the wondrous stories of angels and his mother's filling with the Holy Spirit seemed out of reach. But it didn't take long for John to come around, for him to grasp fully who Jesus was.

STILL NO ONE GREATER

John's disciples delivered his question to Jesus. Jesus then commanded John's followers to go back to John and report, "The blind receive their sight, the lame walk, those with leprosy are cleansed, the deaf hear, the dead are raised, and the poor are told the good news..." (Matt 11:5 CSB). Armed with this information, John's followers began their return trip. However, Jesus was not finished talking about John the Baptist. As John's followers leave, Jesus turns to the crowd and makes this astonishing statement: "Truly I tell you, among those born of women no one greater than John the Baptist has appeared..." (Matt. 11:11 CSB).

No one greater! Jesus said this despite having just heard about John's doubt. Maybe you have doubts this Christmas, too. Maybe you've struggled or even suffered. Maybe you're like John and in prison! And like John, who had ample evidence to trust in Jesus, you still doubt if trusting in him is the right thing. And maybe as a result of your doubt, you feel like you've failed Jesus. You've let him down.

Be encouraged. On the wings of doubt, Jesus still proclaimed John to be one of the greatest. But do you know what else Jesus said? Jesus said at the end of verse 11, "but the least in the kingdom of heaven is greater than [John]" (CSB). Does that cause you to do a double take? Well, you heard right! The least of the followers of Jesus is even greater than John the Baptist. If you follow Jesus, that means you! Be encouraged!

QUESTIONS

1. Do you know any of your family heritage? Who are you related to that is of interest to you?
2. How were Elizabeth (John's mother) and Mary (Jesus's mother) related?
3. If you were in John's situation (Herod's prison), do you think you may have had doubts about Jesus?
4. When Jesus was asked if he was "the one" or if someone else should be expected, what was his reply?
5. Why is the end of Matthew 11:11 important to followers of Jesus?

PRAYER FOR THE DAY

"Father, I thank you that I am not alone in my fears and doubts. In the difficulty of life, sometimes I doubt like John doubted. When I do, Lord, please remind me of Jesus's answer: 'The blind receive their sight, the lame walk, those with leprosy are cleansed, the deaf hear, the dead are raised, and the poor are told the good news....' Thank you for the power of Jesus, which proved he is the ONE."

JOHN THE BAPTIST
NOT WORTHY

December 18th
Light six candles.

THE SUPER-CHRISTIAN?

For years, I (Daniel) had the honor of serving in a local church with a worship pastor named Gary. To this day, he is such a dear friend. Out of many memories I have of Gary, one is of his unique Bible. What made this particular Bible so unique was all the signatures found inside the pages. Over the years, Gary had met many well-known preachers and had collected their autographs in the pages of his Bible. Names like Adrian Rogers, Charles Stanley, Billy Graham, and W.A. Criswell could be found there, just to name a few. He had amassed a collection of signatures from these great men of the 1970s and 1980s who had led our particular convention through some troubled times. These men were (and some still are) giants of the faith.

As well-known as these men are, none of them are as famous as John the Baptist was. When John came out of the wilderness preaching, people came in droves to hear him. Even the religious leaders down in Jerusalem heard the news about John and traveled for miles to meet this rogue preacher and see what all the fuss was about. His message was getting out, and he was having an impact!

A PICTURE OF HUMILITY

Many would let the sort of success and attention John experienced inflate their egos. Not John. He gave us a picture of ongoing humility. He was aware of who he was and who Jesus was. The Gospel of Luke records the words of John as he explains to his followers about the coming Messiah: "… I baptize you with water; but One is coming who is mightier than I, and I am not fit to untie the thong of His sandals" (Luke 3:16).

John intentionally used this picture of humility because, at that time, feet were simply a dirty and detestable part of the human body. Everyone traveled on foot and had to walk on mud and dirt roads littered with animal dung and other unsanitary items. Feet were so disgusting that household servants and slaves were usually the ones to remove dirty sandals from their master's feet before washing them clean. So, when John says he's not fit to untie Jesus's sandal, he was essentially saying, "I am not even worthy to be Jesus's servant or slave."

In spite of John's great success, he maintained a clear perspective on who he was and who Jesus was. When many of his disciples decided to leave him and follow Jesus instead, John humbly said, "He must increase, but I must decrease" (Jn. 3:30).

What is your perspective this Christmas? Maybe you're very successful in business, in ministry, or in life. Have you allowed your success to give you an inflated view of yourself? Or perhaps you feel guilty because you're not a "super-Christian." There is no such person. In my twenty-five-plus years of ministry, I've seen "super-Christians" fall like flies into sin and temptation. I've also seen humble, non-famous pastors lead and shepherd people with the heart of Jesus. They remained focused on who they were and who Jesus is. What about you? Have you managed to maintain a humble self-perspective in light of who Jesus is?

QUESTIONS

1. John was a famous preacher, but what was his attitude once Jesus hit the scene?
2. Do you feel like preachers today have the humility John had? Why or why not?
3. Do you struggle with humility? What does James 4:6 say?
4. Can you think of people in the past who seemed to have it all together but fell into temptation?
5. How do we remind ourselves that we are not "super-Christians"? How can Paul's words in Philippians 3:4-10 be helpful in the quest for humility?

PRAYER FOR THE DAY

"Father, help me remember that Jesus is the only super-Christian. Guard and protect me against pride. Help me find my everything in Jesus. Thank you for examples, like John, who decrease so that Christ may increase."

PART SEVEN

Jesus Christ, God's Magnum Opus

JESUS CHRIST
GOD'S MAGNUM OPUS

December 19th
Light seven candles.

Mary said to the angel, "How can this be, since I am a virgin?" The angel answered and said to her, "The Holy Spirit will come upon you, and the power of the Most High will overshadow you; and for that reason the holy Child shall be called the Son of God."

— *Luke 1:34-35*

GOD'S MAGNUM OPUS

A magnum opus is Latin; it means "great work." It is usually used in conjunction with an artist's or writer's greatest achievement or masterpiece, such as in reference to Victor Hugo's *Les Misérables*. Of all the miraculous births in the Bible, this seventh birth is by far God's magnum opus. God goes beyond the miracle of conception from barrenness; this time, he brings conception from pure virginity. According to a 1990 *LA Times* article, famous talk-show host Larry King said that his fantasy interview would be with Jesus Christ. King said, "I would ask him if he believed that he was born of virgin birth, because whatever the answer is changes or reinforces the world."[1]

VIRGIN BIRTH PROMISED LONG AGO

In Genesis 3:15, God makes a promise to mankind. This verse has been referred to by scholars as the *protoevangelium*, which means "first gospel." This peculiar verse is a promise of the gospel. It says, "And I will put enmity between you and the woman, and between your seed and her seed; He shall bruise you on the head, and you shall bruise him on the heel." God curses the devil when he says that the "seed of the woman" would bruise the head of the serpent. The Hebrew indicates that this bruising is really more of a crushing.[2]

The most interesting thing about this verse is that women don't have seed (as we know today). The seed comes from the man, and the egg is produced by the woman. It is biologically impossible for a woman to have seed, yet this passage clearly teaches it! The prophet Isaiah would later shed light on this verse when he says in Isaiah 7:14, "Therefore the Lord Himself will give you a sign: Behold, a virgin will be with child and bear a son, and she will call His name Immanuel."

When we put this all together with the fact that Immanuel means "God with us," we see Scripture clearly teaching that a virgin woman will produce the Son of God!

A DIVINE ANNOUNCEMENT

In Luke 1:34-35, we see the angel tell Mary she was going to have a son. She instantly says, "'How can this be, since I am a virgin?' The angel answered and said to her, 'The

Holy Spirit will come upon you, and the power of the Most High will overshadow you; and for that reason the holy Child shall be called the Son of God.'"

As in our other birth stories, we see a heavenly messenger prophesying another miraculous birth. The only difference is that this child will actually be the Son of God. Think about it for a minute. If our sons are extensions of us, that makes them by nature human. That means God's son, as an extension of himself, must be divine.

A PROMISE COMES TO FRUITION

After Mary and Joseph arrived in Bethlehem, the Bible records, "While they were there, the days were completed for her to give birth. And she gave birth to her firstborn son; and she wrapped Him in cloths, and laid Him in a manger, because there was no room for them in the inn" (Lk. 2:6-7). There was quite the celebration the night of Jesus's birth, which was announced by an angel to shepherds out in the field. They were told that the Savior, Christ the Lord, had been born. The shepherds found Mary and Joseph as quickly as they could and told them of the angel's message. When Mary heard their story, the Scriptures say that she "… treasured all these things, pondering them in her heart" (Lk. 2:19). Hearing the shepherds that night must have been confirmation for Mary that the miracle was complete. She was the vessel chosen by God to bring forth the most miraculous birth in history. The seventh miraculous birth in the Bible was of her son, Jesus. Surely it is true what Gabriel said to Mary when he first appeared to her: "Greetings favored one! The Lord is with you" (Lk. 1:28). The virgin birth of Jesus demonstrates that nothing is too difficult for God!

QUESTIONS

1. What is a magnum opus? Why would the birth of Jesus be called that?
2. What is unusual about the prophecy of Genesis 3:15 and the seed of the woman?
3. Why do you think Larry King's first question to Jesus would be whether he was actually born of a virgin?
4. What does Immanuel mean?
5. If you had one question that you could ask Jesus, would you ask the same one as Larry King or a different one? Share with your family what that question would be.

PRAYER FOR THE DAY

"God, we thank you for keeping your promises! We thank you for multiple promises in the Bible concerning the birth of the Messiah, and that we can see your plans foreshadowed throughout history. Please help us trust in your plan for our life as you helped Mary and Joseph. We thank you for the miraculous birth of Jesus!"

SONG FOR THE DAY: HARK THE HERALD ANGELS SING (CHARLES WESLEY)

Verse 1

Hark! The herald angels sing,
"Glory to the new-born King!
Peace on earth, and mercy mild,
God and sinners reconciled."

Joyful, all ye nations, rise,
Join the triumph of the skies;
With' th'angelic host proclaim,
"Christ is born in Bethlehem."
Hark! the herald angels sing,
"Glory to the new-born King!"

Verse 2

Christ, by highest heaven adored:
Christ, the everlasting Lord;
Late in time behold him come,
Offspring of the favoured one.
Veiled in flesh, the Godhead see;
Hail, th' incarnate Deity:
Pleased, as man, with men to dwell,
Jesus, our Emmanuel!
Hark! the herald angels sing,
"Glory to the new-born King!"

Verse 3

Hail! the heaven-born Prince of peace!
Hail! the Son of Righteousness!
Light and life to all he brings,
Risen with healing in his wings.
Mild he lays his glory by,
Born that man no more may die,
Born to raise the sons of earth,
Born to give them second birth.
Hark! the herald angels sing,
"Glory to the new-born King!"

JESUS CHRIST
THE MORE COMPLETE SACRIFICE

December 20th
Light seven candles.

But He was pierced through for our transgressions, He was crushed for our iniquities; the chastening for our well-being fell upon Him, and by His scourging we are healed.
— *Isaiah 53:5*

MYRRH — A BABY GIFT?

Christmas is a time of happiness and joy. It's a time to reflect on the birth of the Savior coming into the world. It is also a time to remember why Jesus came, which is why, each year at our (the Martins') home, we hang a nail on the Christmas tree. Matthew 20:28 may sum it up best. In this verse, Jesus says, "… the Son of Man did not come to be served, but to serve, and to give His life a ransom for many." Jesus came to give his life as a ransom. Jesus was born to die.

Do you remember when the wise men visited Mary, Joseph, and Jesus? Scholars differ on exactly when they showed up, but whenever it was, Jesus was definitely a very young child under two years old. When they arrived, they gave Jesus three gifts: gold, frankincense, and myrrh (Matt. 2:11). Gold was a gift given to a king. Frankincense was given to a priest, and myrrh was used for anointing or burial. These gifts were significant. Though given when Jesus was just a child, they pointed ahead to a time when Christ would be king and priest, and when he would die on behalf of his people. The mission of this king-priest was total sacrifice.

MOUNT MORIAH

This Advent book started on Mount Moriah with the story of Abraham and Isaac. Isaac was spared as God provided a ram in a thicket. But later in Israelite history, as mentioned before, Moriah also became the hill where Solomon built the temple. In the temple, sacrifices for the nation were made. Gentiles were only allowed in the outer court of the temple. They weren't allowed near the presence of God inside the Holy of Holies. Only Jews and priests could draw near to God, and only the High Priest (once per year on the Day of Atonement) could enter the Holy of Holies to offer up a sacrifice for the sins of the nation. This sacrifice was weak in that it needed to be repeated year after year. Just as Abraham took his only begotten (Gen. 22:2) to Moriah, God the Father took his only begotten (Jn. 1:14,18) to the public hill of Golgotha. As Isaac carried the tree for the offering (Gen. 22:6), Jesus carried his tree to his death (Jn. 19:17), and in almost prophetic speech, we can hear the words of Abraham to Isaac: "God will provide for Himself the lamb" (Gen. 22:8). Jesus fulfilled all of God's laws perfectly for us (Matt. 5:17). Because of this, he was the spotless lamb of God who could pay the price for our sins on the cross. God provided for us the lamb of God who takes away the sin of the world (Jn. 1:29).

JESUS'S DEATH WAS FOR ALL TO SEE

Jesus's death was public; everyone could see it. Whereas sacrifices were hidden (especially from Gentiles) at the temple, Jesus was publicly sacrificed. The author of Hebrews says it this way: "Therefore Jesus also, that He might sanctify the people through His own blood, suffered outside the gate" (Heb. 13:12). Jesus was crucified outside the gate of Jerusalem on public display. Jesus's last words were "tetelestai," which means "paid in full!" The sin debt was paid, and at that moment, the veil of the temple in the Holy of Holies was torn in two from top to bottom (Matt. 27:51).

Everyone now has access to God. Paul says of Gentiles in Ephesians 2:13, "But now in Christ Jesus you who formerly were far off have been brought near by the blood of Christ." God didn't require Abraham's son to be sacrificed, but because of his great love for us, God the Father willingly sacrificed his son for us. Hebrews 10:12 says, "… but He, having offered one sacrifice for sins for all time, sat down at the right hand of God…."

Philippians 2:5-11 is a famous passage of Scripture known as "The Song of Christ." Consider the power of the following passage today as you remember that the greatest gift ever given to you at Christmas was Jesus:

Have this attitude in yourselves which was also in Christ Jesus, who, although He existed in the form of God, did not regard equality with God a thing to be grasped, but emptied Himself, taking the form of a bond-servant, and being made in the likeness of men. Being found in appearance as a man, He humbled Himself by becoming obedient to the point of death, even death on a cross. For this reason also, God highly exalted Him, and bestowed on Him the name which is above every name, so that at the name of Jesus every knee will bow, of those who are in heaven and on earth and under the earth, and that every tongue will confess that Jesus Christ is Lord, to the glory of God the Father.

Jesus Christ, the exalted Son of God, came "not to be served, but to serve, and to give his life as a ransom for many" (Matt. 20:28 CSB).

QUESTIONS

1. What are some similarities you noticed between the story of Isaac and the story of Jesus?
2. What are some similarities you noticed between Abraham and God the Father?
3. How is the public sacrifice of Jesus different from the sacrifices held inside the temple?
4. Have you ever thought at Christmas-time not just about the birth of Jesus but also the death of Jesus?
5. What does Paul mean when he tells Gentiles that they are no longer "far off" but have been "brought near by the blood of Christ"?

PRAYER FOR THE DAY

"Father, I want to thank you for allowing me to draw near to you because of the blood of Christ. I thank you, Jesus, for keeping all God's laws perfectly for me. I also thank you for shedding

your blood in my place for my sins. Help me remember this Christmas that you came to give your life as a ransom for the sins of the world."

SONG FOR THE DAY: IN CHRIST ALONE (KEITH GETTY)

Verse 1

In Christ alone my hope is found
He is my light, my strength, my song
This Cornerstone, this solid ground
Firm through the fiercest drought and storm
What heights of love, what depths of peace
When fears are stilled, when strivings cease
My Comforter, my All in All
Here in the love of Christ I stand.

Verse 2

In Christ alone, who took on flesh
Fullness of God in helpless babe
This gift of love and righteousness
Scorned by the ones He came to save
'Til on that cross as Jesus died
The wrath of God was satisfied
For every sin on Him was laid
Here in the death of Christ I live.

Verse 3

There in the ground His body lay
Light of the world by darkness slain

Then bursting forth in glorious Day
Up from the grave He rose again
And as He stands in victory
Sin's curse has lost its grip on me
From life's first cry to final breath,
Jesus commands my destiny
No power of hell, no scheme of man,
Can ever pluck me from His hand
Till he returns or calls me home
Here in the power of Christ I'll stand.

Isaac	Scripture Reference	Jesus	Scripture Reference
Mother is Acar/Barren	Genesis 11:29	Mother is Virgin	Matthew 1:18
Birth Promised & Foretold (Theophany)	Genesis 17:9	Birth Promised & Foretold (Angelic Witness)	Luke 1:28-38
The Impossible Son of a Dead Womb	Genesis 17:17 Romans 4:19	The Impossible Son of a Virgin's Womb	Matthew 1:18 Luke 1:34
The Son of the Promise "Only Begotten"	Genesis 17:18-19 Genesis 22:2	The Only Begotten Son of God	John 1:14, 18
Carried His Own Tree for the Burnt Offering	Genesis 22:6	Carried the Slave's Tree to be an Offering	John 19:17 Ephesians 5:2
Isaac is Obedient to the Point of Death	Genesis 22:9-10	Jesus is Obedient to the Point of Death	Philippians 2:8
A Foreshadowing of the Imperfect Sacrificial System on Mt. Moriah "God will provide Himself a lamb."	1 Kings 6-8 2 Chronicles 3:1	Jesus put an end to sacrifice on Mt. Moriah. (God provided a ram for Isaac, not a lamb.) Christ became the Lamb (1 Peter 1:19; John 1:29).	Hebrews 10:12
Isaac is Called a Type of Christ	Hebrews 11:19	The Substance of Fulfilled Prophecy Belongs to Christ	Colossians 2:17

JESUS CHRIST
A NEW LOVE STORY, A NEW NATION

December 21st
Light seven candles.

So the woman left her waterpot, and went into the city and said to the men, "Come, see a man who told me all the things that I have done; this is not the Christ, is it?"
— *John 4:28-29*

SWORN ENEMIES

One of the most famous stories ever written is Shakespeare's *Romeo and Juliet*. The story, of course, is about two families that are sworn enemies. The Capulet and Montague families hate each other. Juliet is a Capulet, and Romeo is a Montague. The problem is that they love each other and want to be together, but their families would never approve! Keep this story in mind.

In the first century world, Jews and Gentiles did not socialize. When Jews would leave a Gentile city, they would shake the dust off their feet. The Gentiles were known as "far off ones" because of their status in the temple precinct. Jews also referred to Gentiles as dogs, which they believed were unclean! Because Gentiles were considered unclean, certain things were deemed proper and improper when coming in to contact with them.

Samaria was a city frowned upon during the time of Jesus. Once the capital city of Israel, Samaria was judged by God in 722 BC when he used the Assyrians to judge the Israelites for their sins. The Assyrians conquered the land and then resettled it with pagans; only some Jews remained (2 Kings 17:24). Those remaining Jews of Samaria intermarried with pagans and were eventually considered foreigners by the pure-bred Jews to the south in Judah.

Because of this history, the Jews in Jesus's time considered the Samaritans unclean and avoided the judged city of Samaria at all costs. In fact, during the time of Jesus, it was common for a Jew passing by Samaria to walk around the city so they would not have to make contact with any unclean Samaritans. But Jesus defied the stigma associated with the Samaritans in his parable of the "Good Samaritan," which would have been considered scandalous! Jesus portrays the pure Jewish priest and the pure Jewish Levite as villains, while the "unclean" Samaritan is the hero (Lk. 10)! Encouraging any sort of intimate dealings between Jews and Samaritans would have made the religious leaders hate Jesus even more than they already did.

ANOTHER WOMAN, ANOTHER WELL

Instead of walking around Samaria, Jesus led his disciples into the heart of Samaria and went directly to a well. But this wasn't just any well. John 4:5-6 says, "So He came to a city of Samaria called Sychar, near the parcel of ground that Jacob gave to his son Joseph; and Jacob's well was there. So Jesus, being wearied from His journey, was sitting thus by the well. It was about the sixth hour."

Remember that Jacob (Israel) was instructed to find a pure-bred bride, and that he found Rachel at the well. As Jesus sat at Jacob's well so many years later, an unclean Samaritan woman walked up to it. But he did something unexpected. He interacted with her. He acknowledged her. He asked her to give him a drink. The woman was astounded. She says in John 4:9, "How is it that You, being a Jew, ask me for a drink since I am a Samaritan woman?" The verse goes on to remind the reader that Jews had "no dealings with Samaritans." Merrill Tenney, a professor of New Testament and Greek, says of this passage: "No Jewish rabbi would have volunteered to carry on a public conversation with a woman, nor would he have deigned to drink from a Samaritan's cup, as she implied in her answer."[1] Jesus broke all the cultural rules by having a conversation with an unclean woman in an unclean town, going so far as to *ask* to drink from her unclean vessel. Jesus was not stopped by Jewish cultural idiosyncrasies. Instead, he offers the woman a relationship, as we see in John 4:10-14:

> Jesus answered and said to her, "If you knew the gift of God, and who it is who says to you, 'Give Me a drink,' you would have asked Him, and He would have given you living water."
>
> She said to Him, "Sir, You have nothing to draw with and the well is deep; where then do You get that living water? You are not greater than our father Jacob, are You, who gave us the well, and drank of it himself and his sons and his cattle?"
>
> Jesus answered and said to her, "Everyone who drinks of this water will thirst again; but whoever drinks of the

water that I will give him shall never thirst; but the water that I will give him will become in him a well of water springing up to eternal life."

Jesus offers this unclean woman eternal life through him. As the conversation continues, Jesus makes it clear that he knows this woman is a sinner. In fact, he knows all about her past (Jn. 4:16-18). In spite of that, Jesus still loves her and wants a relationship with her.

THE NEW ISRAEL, A FORBIDDEN BRIDE

If the Jews in Jesus's time came into contact with anything or anyone unclean, according to the Law, they immediately became unclean as well. However, anything Jesus touched *became* clean. The blood of Christ makes all who believe clean. Paul says that in Christ all the barriers have been broken down (Eph. 2:13). He came seeking to reconcile all nations to God. In Matthew 28:18-20, he commissions the church to preach to "all the nations." The word for nations in these verses is *ta ethne*, from which we derive the word *ethnic*. The church is to preach to *all* ethnicities, to *all* mankind!

The bride Jesus seeks is much different from the bride Jacob sought. Jesus is looking for unclean sinners to *make* clean by his precious blood. He is looking to reconcile to God any who will come to him. His bride consists of believers from every ethnic group! Paul says this in Ephesians 2:14-18:

For He Himself is our peace, who made both groups into one and broke down the barrier of the dividing wall, by abolishing in His flesh the enmity, which is the Law of commandments contained in ordinances, so that in Himself He might make the two into one new man, thus establishing peace, and might reconcile them both in one body to God through the cross, by it having put to death the enmity. And He came and preached peace to you who were far away, and peace to those who were near; for through Him we both have our access in one Spirit to the Father.

The new nation Christ formed is not grounded in ethnicity. Romans 2:28-29 says, "For he is not a Jew who is one outwardly, nor is circumcision that which is outward in the flesh. But he is a Jew who is one inwardly; and circumcision is that which is of the heart, by the Spirit, not by the letter; and his praise is not from men, but from God."

THE BRIDE LOVES HER GROOM

John 4:39-42 says:

> From that city many of the Samaritans believed in Him because of the word of the woman who testified, "He told me all the things that I have done."
>
> So when the Samaritans came to Jesus, they were asking Him to stay with them; and He stayed there two days. Many more believed because of His word; and they were saying to the woman, "It is no longer because of what you said that we believe, for we have heard for ourselves and know that this One is indeed the Savior of the world."

On day six of our readings, we mentioned prophecies from every section of the Old Testament that indicate the Gentile nations would become followers of God. In

Romans 15:9-12, Paul says that all these Scriptures were fulfilled in Christ.

They couldn't keep Romeo and Juliet apart in Shakespeare's play, could they? You can't keep Jesus from His bride, either, even if she lives in Samaria. Jacob may have been able to pick up the stone off the mouth of the well, but the Samaritan woman said to her community, "Come, see a man who told me all the things that I have done; this is not the Christ, is it?"

QUESTIONS:

1. What were some of the names Jews had for Gentiles before the days of Jesus?
2. What are some differences between the bride Jacob looked for and the bride Jesus is looking for?
3. How is *Romeo and Juliet* like the story of Jesus and his bride, the church?
4. How do we know Jesus loves every ethnic group in the world?

PRAYER FOR THE DAY:

"Jesus, thank you so much for your love for all the nations of the world. We thank you for making it possible for anyone to be reconciled to you through the blood of the cross. Help me to be a faithful witness and to never keep the gospel from anyone that looks different from me. Thank you for making your church pure through your shed blood."

SONG FOR THE DAY: O COME, O COME, EMMANUEL (TRANS. JOHN MASON NEALE)

O come, O come, Emmanuel
And ransom captive Israel
That mourns in lonely exile here
Until the Son of God appear
Rejoice, rejoice, Emmanuel
Shall come to thee, O Israel

O come, Thou Rod of Jesse, free
Thine own from Satan's tyranny
From depths of Hell Thy people save
And give them victory o'er the grave
Rejoice, rejoice, Emmanuel
Shall come to thee, o Israel

O come, Thou Day-Spring
Come and cheer
Our spirits by Thine advent here
Disperse the gloomy clouds of night
And death's dark shadows put to flight
Rejoice, rejoice, Emmanuel
Shall come to thee, o Israel

O come, Thou Key of David, come
And open wide our heavenly home
Make safe the way that leads on high
And close the path to misery
Rejoice, rejoice, Emmanuel
Shall come to thee, o Israel

O come, O come, Thou Lord of might

Who to Thy tribes, on Sinai's height
In ancient times did'st give the Law
In cloud, and majesty and awe
Rejoice, rejoice, Emmanuel
Shall come to thee, o Israel

Jacob	Scripture Reference	Jesus	Scripture Reference
Mother is Acar/Barren	Genesis 25:21	Mother is Virgin	Matthew 1:18
Divine Announcement (Theophany)	Genesis 25:23	Divine Announcement	Luke 1:31
Father of the Old, Ethnic Israel	Genesis 32:28	Father of the New, Spiritual Israel	Matthew 21:43 Romans 2:28-29
Hated by Brother (Later Reconciled)	Genesis 27:41 Genesis 33:4	Despised by Brothers Who Didn't Believe (James Later Believed)	John 7:2-5 Galatians 1:19
Meets Bride at Well in Samaria Bride/Nation to be pure	Genesis 28:1-2 Genesis 29:10-11	Meets Bride (the Church) at Samaria; Impure Becomes Pure	John 4:7-10
Isaiah 54:1 – Barren/Acar Zion Will Stretch Out Her Tents (Gentile Inclusion Implied)	Isaiah 54:1-6	Christ Stretched the Tents to Include "ta ethne"	Matthew 28:18-20 Romans 2, 4, 11 Galatians 3 Ephesians 2:14-15 etc.
His Children Are Recognized by His Name, "Sons of Israel"	Exodus 1:7, 9 etc.	His Children (the New Israel) Called by His Name, "Sons of God"/Christians	John 1:12 1 Peter 4:16
Old Nation Establishes Court of Gentiles with Stiff Penalties	Acts 21:29	New Nation Makes Place of Propitiation Public Through Christ	Matthew 17:51 Romans 3:25 Hebrews 13:12

JESUS CHRIST
THE ULTIMATE FORGIVER

December 22nd
Light seven candles.

When they came to the place called The Skull, there they crucified Him and the criminals, one on the right and the other on the left. But Jesus was saying, "Father, forgive them; for they do not know what they are doing."
— Luke 23:33-34

FORGIVENESS DEFINED

The Greek word *aphiemi* means "forgive." In classical Greek, in its basic form, this word meant "to send off" or "to send away." Greek writers used this word in a variety of ways, referring to anything from an archer releasing arrows, to ending a meeting, to losing a ship to the sea. This word is sometimes translated as "divorce," as one person sends the other away.[1]

When Joseph forgave his brothers, he took their crimes against him, his animosity, his desire for justice, and any urges for revenge and sent them away. As an archer releases arrows from his bow, Joseph launched those thoughts, emotions, and injustices into oblivion. That is forgiveness.

FORGIVENESS PERSONIFIED

An even greater example of a forgiver is THE forgiver, Jesus. Whereas Joseph amazingly forgave his ten brothers for their betrayal, Jesus forgives billions — including you and me — for a myriad of egregious sins. As Paul and Barnabas so faithfully proclaimed, "Therefore, my friends, I want you to know that through Jesus the forgiveness of sins is proclaimed to you" (Acts 13:38 NIV).

Just as Joseph was the only man who could forgive the ten brothers' sins against him, only God can forgive our sins against him. Jesus came as God in the flesh to do just that (and so much more). In Mark 2, we see Jesus teaching in a crowded house. Four men brought their paralyzed friend to Jesus for healing. Facing the obstacle of an intensely crowded home, they cut a hole in the roof and lowered their friend to lay at the feet of Jesus. Mark records, "Seeing their faith, Jesus told the paralytic, 'Son, your sins are forgiven'" (Mark 2:5 CSB). The religious leaders seated close to Jesus were immediately stirred and questioned Jesus in their hearts since they rightly knew that no one could forgive sins but God alone. Which was exactly the point! They just didn't realize God was standing right in front of them.

FORGIVENESS ORDAINED

You may have heard this famous statement Joseph made to his brothers: "You planned evil against me; God planned it for good..." (Genesis 50:20 CSB). Joseph recognized that in order for God's people to be rescued from the famine, he had to experience injustice at the hands of his brothers and then return that injustice with forgiveness. In an even more powerful way, Jesus's death on the cross — his forgiveness of us — was ordained by God in order for God's people to be rescued from sin.

When we trust in Jesus as Lord and Savior, seek his forgiveness, and commit our life to following him, the Bible says he truly forgives us. The Apostle John writes, "If we confess our sins, he is faithful and righteous to forgive us our sins and cleanse us from all unrighteousness." (1 Jn. 1:9 CSB). He takes our sins, and he "sends them away." Just imagine all our sins as arrows being shot away from the bow of the cross! The psalmist writes, "As far as the east is from the west, so far has he removed our transgressions from us" (Ps. 103:12 CSB).

Just as Joseph's brothers did not deserve Joseph's mercy, neither do we deserve the mercy of God. We don't merit forgiveness. Yet, because of his great love, he forgives us.

FORGIVENESS EXTREME

As you read through the pages of history in Scripture, you encounter some rather extreme sinners. Moses murdered and lived as a fugitive. David committed adultery with a close friend's wife, and then he conspired to murder this same friend to cover his sin, which resulted in an unwanted pregnancy. His conspiracy to murder resulted in the death of his friend. Paul led the way in the persecution of God's people; he was a true enemy of God. Yet, in all these cases, the Scriptures testify that God forgave them as they turned from sin and trusted in him.

This extreme forgiveness through Jesus lies at the heart

of Christmas. Yes, we celebrate the birth of Jesus. But why? Because he is the hope of life, purpose, joy, and *forgiveness*! Are you forgiven by God right now? Have you turned your life over to Jesus and trusted in him? We encourage you to truly live out the heart of Christmas by embracing Jesus and his forgiveness.

QUESTIONS

1. How would you explain forgiveness to a six-year-old?
2. Have you done some things in your life that you're not sure God will forgive?
3. Have you turned your life over to Jesus and trusted in him for forgiveness?
4. Is there someone you need to forgive so God can continue to accomplish his purpose in your life?

PRAYER FOR THE DAY

"Jesus, I ask for your forgiveness. I know I've sinned, and ultimately, all my sin is against you. Thank you for going to the cross for me. Thank you for bearing my sin and paying the price for my forgiveness."

SONG FOR THE DAY: COME THOU LONG EXPECTED JESUS (CHARLES WESLEY)

Come, Thou long expected Jesus
Born to set Thy people free;
From our fears and sins release us,
Let us find our rest in Thee.
Israel's strength and consolation,

Hope of all the earth Thou art;
Dear desire of every nation,
Joy of every longing heart.

Born Thy people to deliver,
Born a child and yet a King,
Born to reign in us forever,
Now Thy gracious kingdom bring.
By Thine own eternal Spirit
Rule in all our hearts alone;
By Thine all sufficient merit,
Raise us to Thy glorious throne.

By Thine all sufficient merit,
Raise us to Thy glorious throne.

Joseph	Scripture Reference	Jesus	Scripture Reference
Mother is Acar/Barren	Genesis 29:31	Mother is Virgin	Matthew 1:18
Sold for Price of a Slave	Genesis 37:28	Sold for Price of a Slave	Matthew 26:15
Brothers Reconciled, Redeemed, & Raised to Honor	Genesis 32:28	Brothers Reconciled, Redeemed, & Raised to Honor	John 21:15-18
Fed Bread to the Multitudes; 7-Year Shortage	Genesis 41:40-49	Fed Bread to the Multitudes; 7 Baskets Left Over	Matthew 15:37
Shepherd	Genesis 37:2	Calls Himself the "Good Shepherd"	John 10:11-14
Taken to Egypt & Life is Spared	Genesis 37:28	Taken to Egypt & Life is Spared	Matthew 2:13
Ministry Begins at 30 Years Old	Genesis 41:38	Ministry Begins at (About) 30 Years Old	Luke 3:23
Filled with the Spirit of God	Genesis 41:38	Filled with the Spirit of God	Luke 4:1
Loved Freely	Genesis 45:15	Loved Freely	John 13:34
Resisted the Most Difficult Temptations	Genesis 39:8-9	Resisted All Temptations	Hebrews 4:15

Joseph vs. Jesus Chart Continued ...

Joseph vs. Jesus Chart Continued . . .			
Joseph	**Scripture Reference**	**Jesus**	**Scripture Reference**
Given Visions of the Future	Genesis 37:6	Revealed Future/ Predicted Temple Destruction	Matthew 24:3
Hated for Teachings	Genesis 37:8	Hated for Teachings	John 7:7
Falsely Accused	Genesis 39:4	Falsely Accused	Mark 14:56
Silent Before Accuser	Genesis 39:20	Silent Before Accuser	Mark 15:4
Condemned Between 2 Prisoners; 1 Received Life from Joseph's Vision; 1 Received Death	Genesis 40	Condemned Between 2 Prisoners; 1 Received Life from Jesus; 1 Received Death	Luke 23:39-43
Not Recognized by His Own Brothers	Genesis 42:8	Not Recognized by His Own People	John 1:5
Became a Servant	Genesis 39:4	Became a Servant for Mankind	Philippians 2:7
Became Lord of Egypt after Resurrected to His Family	Genesis 39:20	Will Return Lord of All; Resurrected from the Dead	Mark 15:4

JESUS CHRIST
THE PERFECT SAVIOR

December 23rd
Light seven candles.

But Jesus was saying, "Father, forgive them; for they do not know what they are doing."
— *Luke 23:34*

THE REAL SUPERMAN

If you watch superhero movies, you know there is none tougher than the DC comic hero, Superman! Superman stands out among his DC peers as the man that can put an end to trouble. In the movie *Justice League*, he is clearly the strongest of the superheroes. He even conquers death by resurrection! (We think they stole that idea from somewhere else.)

Interestingly, the story of Superman starts on Krypton. His father, Jor-El, unable to save his home planet, sends his only son to earth. Under the yellow sun of the earth, Superman draws his superhuman strength. Superman, like Samson in the Old Testament, is a savior of sorts. He has the ability to save people by fighting battles on their behalf. He saves their physical bodies so they might live a little while longer. But he has no way to save their souls. Both Samson (in the real world) and Superman (in the comic world) can only save the body. When it comes to saving the whole man, both Samson and Superman are found wanting.

A few days ago, you learned that Samson's name means "sunny." The only other person referred to as the "sun" in the Bible is Jesus. There is a prophecy in Malachi 4:2 that says, "But for you who fear My name, the sun of righteousness will rise with healing in its wings; and you will go forth and skip about like calves from the stall." Jesus is the fulfillment of this prophecy. Zacharias, the father of John the Baptist, says in Luke 1:78, "Because of the tender mercy of our God, with which the Sunrise from on high will visit us..." Jesus is that illuminating sunlight from God! He is, according to John, "the true Light which, coming into the world, enlightens every man" (Jn. 1:9). This new Sun (Jesus) proves to be a better Savior than either Samson or Superman.

THE PERFECT SAVIOR

While the prophecy about Samson said that he would "begin to save Israel from the hand of the Philistines," Jesus's saving of his people is complete and includes both body and soul! Not only does Jesus save our souls through the sacrifice he made for us on the cross, but he also promises to raise the dead bodies of all the saints who have passed on before his return. As believers, we typically only think of our souls being saved when we die, but there is much more to Christ's saving power. The perfect Savior is not going to lose anything to the devil. 1 John 3:8

says, "The Son of God appeared for this purpose, to destroy the works of the devil." The Bible is clear that the wages of sin are both physical and spiritual death. Jesus came to rescue us from both. He clearly speaks to both types of saving that human beings need. He pictures these as necessary awakenings that precede eternal life. In John 5:25-29, Jesus says:

> Truly, truly, I say to you, an hour is coming and now is, when the dead will hear the voice of the Son of God, and those who hear will live. For just as the Father has life in Himself, even so He gave to the Son also to have life in Himself; and He gave Him authority to execute judgment, because He is the Son of Man. Do not marvel at this; for an hour is coming, in which all who are in the tombs will hear His voice, and will come forth; those who did the good deeds to a resurrection of life, those who committed the evil deeds to a resurrection of judgment.

If you have trusted in Christ as your Savior, then breathe a sigh of relief. You don't have to do anything to earn God's approval. Jesus paid your sin debt in full. Hebrews 10:12 (ESV) says, "But when Christ had offered for all time a single sacrifice for sins, he sat down at the right hand of God." Christians are saved both body and soul to spend eternity with Jesus.

REDEMPTION, NOT REVENGE

Samson's last words with arms outstretched as he sacrificed himself were cries to God asking for vengeance for the loss of his eyes. Jesus, with arms outstretched, looked at the sinners murdering him and said, "Father, forgive them; for they do not know what they are doing"

(Lk. 23:34). One savior killed in revenge, while the other Savior was killed in order to redeem. One savior could only save the mortal bodies of some of his people. The other Savior gathers unto himself people from all nations and then promises to save their bodies *and* souls. The true Superman is Jesus. Have you trusted the perfect Savior?

QUESTIONS

1. What similarities do you see between Samson, Superman, and Jesus?
2. What makes Jesus a better Savior than both Samson and Superman?
3. Why is the sun important for all three of these characters?
4. How were the deaths of Samson and Jesus similar? How did they differ?
5. Have you trusted in Jesus to save both your soul and your body?

PRAYER FOR THE DAY

"Thank you, Jesus, for being the perfect Savior. I thank you for saving my soul and promising to one day make my body perfect and brand new. I thank you that you are a God of redemption and not revenge. Help me to always be forgiving and kind to those around me."

SONG FOR THE DAY: HE SHALL REIGN
FOREVERMORE (CHRIS TOMLIN)

In the bleak mid-winter
All creation groans,
For a world in darkness
Frozen like a stone
Light is breaking, in a stable for a throne

And He shall reign forevermore, forevermore
And He shall reign forevermore, forevermore

Unto us a Child is born
The King of kings and Lord of lords
And He shall reign forevermore, forevermore

If I were a wise man
I would travel far
If I were a shepherd,
I would do my part, but poor as
I am I will give to Him my heart

And He shall reign Forevermore, forevermore
And He shall reign Forevermore, forevermore

Unto us a Child is born
The King of kings and Lord of lords
And He shall reign Forevermore, forevermore

Here within a manger lies
The One who made the
Starry skies
This baby born for sacrifice

Christ, the Messiah!
Into our hopes, into our fears
The Savior of the world appears
The promise of eternal years
Christ, the Messiah!

And He shall reign Forevermore, forevermore
And He shall reign Forevermore, forevermore
And He shall reign Forevermore, forevermore
And He shall reign Forevermore, forevermore

Unto us a Child is born
The King of kings and Lord of lords
And He shall reign Forevermore, forevermore

He shall reign
He shall reign
He shall reign

Samson	Scripture Reference	Jesus	Scripture Reference
Mother is Acar/Barren	Judges 13:2	Mother is Virgin	Matthew 1:18
Divine Announcement	Judges 13:3	Divine Announcement	Luke 1:28-31
Angel Proclaims He Will Save His People	Judges 13:5	Angel Proclaims He Will Save His People From Sins	Matthew 1:21
Name Means "Sunny" or "Sun-like."	BDB 1039	He is the "Sun of Righteousness" and "the Sunrise from on high."	Malachi 4:2 John 1:5 Luke 1:78
Set Apart From the Womb (Nazirite)	Judges 13:5	Set Apart From the Womb	Matthew 1:20
Betrayed by Intimate Friend	Judges 16:18	Betrayed by Intimate Friend	Matthew 26:49-50
Betrayed for a Certain Price of Silver	Judges 16:5	Betrayed for 30 Pieces of Silver	Matthew 26:15
Interrogated 4x Consecutively; Questioned About Source of Power	Judges 16:6-18	Interrogated 4x Consecutively; Questioned About Source of Power	Luke 22:66-23:25
Delivered More of His People & Conquered More of His Foe in Death Rather than in Life	Judges 16:30	Delivered His People Through Death on a Cross	2 Corinthians 5:19
Laid Down Life, No One Took It	Judges 16:30	Laid Down Life, No One Took It	John 10:17-18
Died with Arms Outstretched, Seeking Revenge	Judges 16:28-29	Died (Crucified) with Arms Outstretched, Granting Forgiveness	Matthew 27:35 Luke 23:34

JESUS CHRIST
THE PERFECT HIGH PRIEST

December 24th
Light seven candles.

"... but Jesus, on the other hand, because He continues forever, holds His priesthood permanently. Therefore He is able also to save forever those who draw near to God through Him, since He always lives to make intercession for them."
— *Hebrews 7:24-25*

THE ROLE OF A PRIEST

Samuel served faithfully as a priest; his role included approaching God on behalf of God's people. He offered sacrifices on behalf of the Israelites and interceded for them through prayer. As an ambassador, when the people demanded a king, Samuel took their demand to God. He anointed both King Saul and King David as God directed him.

THE OLD TESTAMENT HIGH PRIEST

In the Old Testament, the high priest was the only person who, once per year on the Day of Atonement, could enter the Holy of Holies to present the sacrifice to God on the mercy seat of the Ark of the Covenant. This was an incredibly high honor and a critical event in the spiritual life of Old Testament Israel.

God had sovereignly declared that the priests of the Old Testament would come from the tribe of Levi. Aaron, Moses's brother, served as the first high priest within the tabernacle. All the high priests to follow would offer that one sacrifice per year on behalf of the people to God. The problem was that the sacrifices those high priests offered were merely symbolic and had no real power in and of themselves. They were carried out as a reminder to the people of their sin. The author of Hebrews teaches us this as he writes, "But in the sacrifices there is a reminder of sins year after year. For it is impossible for the blood of bulls and goats to take away sins" (Heb. 10:3-4 CSB). As a result, these high priests — including Samuel — risked their lives year in and year out in the presence of God to offer these impotent sacrifices.

THE GREAT HIGH PRIEST

The New Testament is clear that Jesus is not only Messiah and King but also Priest. The author of Hebrews states, "For we do not have a high priest who is unable to sympathize with our weaknesses, but one who has been tempted in every way as we are, yet without sin" (Heb. 4:15 CSB). Jesus is our ultimate representative to God the Father as he became fully human on the first Christmas. Sinless and eternal, he proved to be the greater High Priest. The Old

Testament priests, prior to offering sacrifices for the people, had to first offer one for themselves and their sin. Jesus, however, was sinless, and no sacrifice was required of him. Also, the Old Testament priests would serve until they died and were replaced by a new high priest. Often, these high priests were not passionately committed to God; Samuel was an exception. Jesus, however, is eternal. He will never retire or be replaced. Again, the author of Hebrews writes, "Now many have become Levitical priests, since they are prevented by death from remaining in office... He doesn't need to offer sacrifices every day, as high priests do — first for their own sins, then for those of the people. He did this once for all when he offered himself" (Heb. 7:23, 27 CSB).

THE HIGH PRIEST WHO INTERCEDES

When I (Daniel) was a baby, we travelled from Nashville to East Tennessee to see family for Christmas. This was long before car seats and seat-belt laws, so I was happily riding along on my mother's lap. Snow and ice had begun to accumulate as we drove along Interstate 24. Suddenly, my dad hit a patch of ice, and the car skidded sideways off the road. As the car collided with a guardrail, my mother threw her body between me and the front dashboard and leaned over me to shield me from any impact. The guardrail stopped our car. My mother was thrown into the dashboard and windshield. Her back and head took the brunt of the impact. By God's grace, she emerged only with bruising and a mild concussion. I, on the other hand, was perfectly fine. My mother had interceded and mediated for me. She placed herself between me and harm.

As Jesus represents us to the Father, he consistently intercedes for us; he places himself between us and the wrath of God. Hebrews 7:25 (CSB) tells us, "He always lives to intercede for them." Paul says, "For there is one God, and one mediator also between God and men, the man Christ Jesus" (1 Tim. 2:5). When Jesus shields us from the judgment we deserve, he also makes a way for God to impart to us the grace we need. This is what the cross demonstrates. Jesus, as our mediator and intercessor, absorbs the wrath of God we deserve so that, through forgiveness, we are free to embrace and enjoy God's grace and mercy.

QUESTIONS

1. What is the role of a priest?
2. Has anyone ever interceded for you? If so, how?
3. What are some things that make Jesus a great high priest?
4. Have you received the mercy and grace that only Christ can give?

PRAYER FOR THE DAY

"Jesus, thank you for interceding for me. I know your sacrifice did not begin for me at the cross but at that first Christmas. Your love for me is overwhelming. Empower me today to live in a way that honors your intercession for me."

SONG FOR THE DAY: OH COME LET US ADORE HIM (JOHN FRANCIS WADE)

O come, all ye faithful,
Joyful and triumphant,
O come ye, O come ye to Bethlehem!
Come and behold Him,
Born the King of Angels!
O come let us adore Him,
O come let us adore Him,
O come let us adore Him,
Christ the Lord!

God of God,
Light of Light,
Lo! He abhors not the Virgin's womb;
Very God,
Begotten, not created.

O come, all ye faithful,
Joyful and triumphant,
O come ye, O come ye to Bethlehem!
Come and behold Him,
Born the King of Angels!
O come let us adore Him,
O come let us adore Him,
O come let us adore Him,
Christ the Lord!

See how the shepherds
Summoned to His cradle,
Leaving their flocks, draw nigh to gaze!
We, too, will thither
Bend our hearts' oblations.

O come, all ye faithful,
Joyful and triumphant,
O come ye, O come ye to Bethlehem!
Come and behold Him,
Born the King of Angels!
O come let us adore Him,
O come let us adore Him,
O come let us adore Him,
Christ the Lord!

Lo, star-led chieftains,
Magi, Christ adoring,
Offer Him incense, gold and myrrh;
We to the Christ-child
Bring our hearts' oblations

O come, all ye faithful,
Joyful and triumphant,
O come ye, O come ye to Bethlehem!
Come and behold Him,
Born the King of Angels!
O come let us adore Him,
O come let us adore Him,
O come let us adore Him,
Christ the Lord!

Child, for us sinners,
Poor and in the manger,
Fain we embrace Thee with love and awe;
Who would not love Thee,
Loving us so dearly?

O come, all ye faithful,
Joyful and triumphant,
O come ye, O come ye to Bethlehem!
Come and behold Him,
Born the King of Angels!
O come let us adore Him,
O come let us adore Him,
O come let us adore Him,
Christ the Lord!

Sing, choirs of angels,
Sing in exultation,
O sing, all ye citizens of heaven above!
"Glory to God,
In the highest!"

O come, all ye faithful,
Joyful and triumphant,
O come ye, O come ye to Bethlehem!
Come and behold Him,
Born the King of Angels!
O come let us adore Him,
O come let us adore Him,
O come let us adore Him,
Christ the Lord!

Yea, Lord, we greet Thee,
Born this happy morning,
Jesus, to Thee be all glory given;
Word of the Father,
Now in flesh appearing!

O come, all ye faithful,
Joyful and triumphant,
O come ye, O come ye to Bethlehem!
Come and behold Him,
Born the King of Angels!
O come let us adore Him,
O come let us adore Him,
O come let us adore Him,
Christ the Lord!

Samuel	Scripture Reference	Jesus	Scripture Reference
Mother is Acar/Barren	1 Samuel 1:6; 2:5	Mother is Virgin	Matthew 1:18
Imperfect High Priest	Romans 3:23	Perfect High Priest	Hebrews 5:9
Anoints 1st King of Israel & First King of Judah (David)	1 Samuel 10:1 1 Samuel 16:12-13	Anointed as Eternal King by His Father (Levi-Judah Anomaly)	Hebrews 1:6-8 Psalm 110
Judge, Priest, Prophet	1 Samuel 7:6, 15 1 Samuel 2:18 1 Samuel 3:20	Judge, Priest, Prophet	Judge: Acts 17:31 Priest: Hebrews 4:14 Prophet: John 6:14
Was Said to be "Growing in stature and in favor with the Lord and with men."	Genesis 37:2	Jesus "kept increasing in wisdom and stature and in favor with God and men."	Luke 2:52
Itinerant Preaching Ministry	1 Samuel 7:16	Itinerant Preaching Ministry	Matthew - John
People Rejected Preaching & Reign of God	1 Samuel 8:7	People Rejected Preaching & Reign of God	John 19:6
Temporarily Raised from the Dead	1 Samuel 28:13-17	Permanently Raised from the Dead	Matthew 28:18
Anoints 1st King of Judah (David)	1 Samuel 16:13	Last King of Judah	John 19:19
Hannah Prayed Fervently in the Temple for a Son	1 Samuel 1:9	Anna (Hannah in Hebrew) Prayed Fervently in the Temple for the Messiah	Luke 2:36-38
Dedicated to the Lord	1 Samuel 1:28	Dedicated to the Lord	Luke 2:23
The similarities between the first chapters of 1 Samuel and Luke 3 are striking!	Hannah prays for Samuel's birth. Samuel left behind at the Tabernacle. Hannah's Song.		Anna prays for Jesus's birth. Jesus left behind at the Temple. Mary's Magnificat.

JESUS CHRIST
THE ONE

December 25th
Light seven candles.

*For my eyes have seen Your salvation, which You have prepared
in the presence of all peoples, A Light of Revelation to the
Gentiles, and the glory of your people Israel.*

— *Luke 2:30-32*

ALL ABOUT ONE

Jesus paid John the Baptist the highest compliment when
he said, "I say to you, among those born among women
there is no one greater than John" (Lk. 7:28). John was
greater than Isaac, the son promised to Abraham. He was
greater than Jacob, despite Jacob becoming Israel's name-
sake. And he was greater than Joseph, who climbed the
ranks in Egypt from a slave to the second-in-command of
the most powerful nation on earth at the time. Samuel, the
great prophet and priest who anointed kings, who served
God faithfully his entire life, was still not as great as John.
Even the great judge Samson, who was unsurpassed in

human strength, was inferior to John the Baptist in Jesus's eyes.

As we previously discussed, John had quite a few followers when Jesus came along, but he readily acknowledged that the One, Jesus, was greater than him. Quickly, many of John's followers began to follow Jesus instead of John. However, instead of responding with pride or jealousy, John simply said, "He must increase, but I must decrease" (Jn. 3:30).

John knew there is no one like Jesus. Why? Because He isn't *just* a man. He is also God. All the great men we have talked about prepared the world for the coming of Jesus, the One.

REJOICE

The night the angels sang "glory to God in the highest" in the presence of the shepherds, they did so because they had just witnessed the mystery of centuries unveiled. The question of how God would redeem creation had finally been answered. The angels, with the greatest view of the second greatest moment in history (second to the resurrection), watched as God confined himself to flesh and presented himself to the world as an infant in the young virgin's arms.

IMMANUEL

The Apostle Matthew quotes from the prophet Isaiah when he writes, "Behold, the virgin shall be with child and shall bear a Son, and they shall call His name Immanuel, which translated means, 'God with us'" (Matt. 1:23). This is Christmas: God has come in the flesh to rescue us from our bondage to sin and death, to rescue creation from the

Fall, and to establish his kingdom here on earth. Christmas is the celebration of the coming of our Savior. He is our only hope, and he is all the hope we need. Merry Christmas!

QUESTIONS

1. How can you truly hope in Jesus more this Christmas?
2. What in your life are you treating as though it were greater than Jesus?
3. With whom can you share the true meaning of Christmas this season?

PRAYER FOR THE DAY

"Jesus, I praise you above all. Of all the things good in my life, none compares to you. Thank you for loving us so much that you chose to become one of us in order to set us free. Lord, help me today to live in your freedom and to truly make you number one in my life. You deserve that and so much more."

SONG FOR THE DAY: O HOLY NIGHT (TRANS. JOHN SULLIVAN DWIGHT)

O Holy Night! The stars are brightly shining
It is the night of the dear Saviour's birth

Long lay the world in sin and error pining
Till He appeared and the soul felt its worth
A thrill of hope the weary world rejoices
For yonder breaks a new and glorious morn
Fall on your knees! Oh, hear the angel voices!

O night divine, the night when Christ was born
O night, O Holy Night, O night divine!
O night, O Holy Night, O night divine!

Led by the light of faith serenely beaming
With glowing hearts by His cradle we stand
O'er the world a star is sweetly gleaming
Now come the wisemen from out of the Orient land
The King of kings lay thus in lowly manger
In all our trials born to be our friend
He knows our need, our weakness is no stranger
Behold your King! Before him lowly bend!
Behold your King! Before him lowly bend!

Truly He taught us to love one another
His law is love and His gospel is peace
Chains he shall break, for the slave is our brother
And in his name all oppression shall cease
Sweet hymns of joy in grateful chorus raise we
With all our hearts we praise His holy name
Christ is the Lord! Then ever, ever praise we
His power and glory ever more proclaim!
His power and glory ever more proclaim!

John	Scripture Reference	Jesus	Scripture Reference
Mother is Acar/Barren	Luke 1:7	Mother is Virgin	Matthew 1:18
Prophet	Matthew 11:9	THE Prophet	Matthew 13:57 Acts 3:22
Priest	Mark 1	Perfect Priest	Hebrews 7:25-28
Sacrifice	Matthew 14	Perfect Sacrifice	Hebrews 10:14-24
Judge/Nazirite	Mark 1	Perfect Savior	John 19:30
Filled with the Spirit	Genesis 41:38 Luke 1:19	Full of the Spirit	Luke 4:1 John 3:34
Anointed the King	Mark 1:9	Jesus is THE King	Luke 23:3 Mark 14:61-62
Culmination of Old Covenant; Mistaken for "the Christ."	Luke 3:15	True Fulfillment of Abrahamic Covenant	Galatians 3:29
Greatest Man Born Among Women (Old Covenant)	Matthew 11:11	Greatest Man Born Ever, Fulfills All of the Law and the Prophets!	Matthew 5:17

ENDNOTES

Introduction

1. Brown, F., Driver, S. R., Briggs, C. A., & Gesenius, W. (1906). *A Hebrew and English lexicon of the Old Testament with an appendix containing the Biblical Aramaic* (p. 785). Oxford, England: Clarendon Press.

December 1st
Isaac the Sacrifice: Old People Having Children?

1. Farmer, B. (2007, August 20). "UK woman, 59, world's oldest natural mother." Retrieved 2020 from https://www.telegraph.co.uk/news/uknews/1560739/UK-woman-59-worlds-oldest-natural-mother.html.

December 3rd
Isaac the Sacrifice: The Lord Provides

1. Sailhamer, J. (1990). Genesis. In J. Sailhamer, W. C. Kaiser, R. L. Harris, & R. Allen (Authors), *Genesis, Exodus, Leviticus, Numbers* (pp. 167-168). Grand Rapids, MI: Zondervan.

December 6th
Jacob the Nation: Peniel/The Face of God

1. Swindoll, C. R. (2002). *Paul: A man of grace and grit: Profiles in character* (p. 2). Nashville, TN: W Pub. Group.
2. Collins, B. (2017, January 17). "Lessons In Conquering Failure From Abraham Lincoln." Retrieved 2020 from https://www.forbes.com/sites/bryancollinseurope/2019/01/17/lessons-in-conquering-failure-from-abraham-lincoln/.
3. NPR Staff. (2012, February 20). "Forget Lincoln Logs: A Tower Of Books To Honor Abe." Retrieved 2020, from https://www.npr.org/2012/02/20/147062501/forget-lincoln-logs-a-tower-of-books-to-honor-abe.

December 10th
Samson the Savior: Sunny Power

1. "The Sun's Energy." (n.d.). Retrieved July 2, 2020, from https://ag.tennessee.edu/solar/Pages/What Is Solar Energy/Sun's Energy.aspx.
2. Brown, F., Driver, S. R., Briggs, C. A., & Gesenius, W. (1906). *A Hebrew and English lexicon*

of the Old Testament with an appendix containing the Biblical Aramaic (p. 1039). Oxford, England: Clarendon Press.

December 11th
Samson the Savior: Strength Becomes Weakness

1. Sukhadwala, I. (2007, November 20). "Man kills lion hyenas kill man." Retrieved 2020 from https://bigcatrescue.org/man-kills-lion-hyenas-kill-man/.

December 19th
Jesus Christ: God's Magnum Opus

1. "SHORT TAKES: King's Fantasy Interview? Jesus." Los Angeles Times, October 15, 1990. https://www.latimes.com/archives/la-xpm-1990-10-15-ca-2099-story.html.
2. Sailhamer, J. (1990). Genesis. In J. Sailhamer, W. C. Kaiser, R. L. Harris, & R. Allen (Authors), *Genesis, Exodus, Leviticus, Numbers* (p. 55). Grand Rapids, MI: Zondervan.

December 21st
Jesus Christ: A New Love Story, a New Nation

1. Tenney, M. (1981). *The Expositor's Bible Commentary: John* (Vol. 5, p. 54). Grand Rapids, MI: Zondervan Pub. House.

December 22nd
Jesus Christ: The Ultimate Forgiver

1. Gilbrant, T. (1986). *The New Testament Greek-English dictionary: Alpha-Gamma* (pp. 503-504) (R. Harris, Ed.). Springfield, MO: Complete Biblical Library.

ACKNOWLEDGMENTS

We would both like to thank our families for their unending support to our personal lives and ministries at Canaan Baptist Church. Also, thank you to our church family at Canaan! It is an honor to build the Kingdom of God with you! We are excited to celebrate Advent in a special way with you through this book. We want to thank our many friends for taking the time to read, reflect, critique and encourage us along the way. Thank you Rick Hedger, Stephen Andrews, Matt Easter, Heather Kaufmann, Mark Lanting, and John Yeats for pre-reading this work and making helpful suggestions. Thank you to Brianna Boes for her design, editing, and layout work. Finally, thank you to Chloe Boes for her hard work on the chapter art for this book. She has been a gift to this project.

ABOUT MARTIN WINSLOW

Martin Winslow is the Pastor of Families/Children and Missions at Canaan Baptist Church in St. Louis, Missouri. With a passion for Christian education, church planting and the poor, Martin has co-founded three Christian schools (Bethlehem Christian Academy). Two schools are in Zambia and one in the 10/40 window of West Africa. Martin is also the author of the blog www.nextgenerationfaithfulness.com.

Martin has a Bachelor's in Biblical Studies from Southwest Baptist University and a Master's in Biblical Languages from Midwestern Baptist Theological Seminary. Martin was married in 1998 to Amy and has five children: Noah, Anna, Emma, Laura, and Nati.

ABOUT DANIEL CARR

Daniel Carr is the Senior Pastor of Canaan Baptist Church in St. Louis, Missouri and an adjunct professor of Old and New Testaments at Missouri Baptist University. He is a graduate of the United States Military Academy at West Point with a B.S. in Mechanical Engineering, and a graduate of The Southern Baptist Theological Seminary with an MDiv from the Billy Graham School of Evangelism and Missions. He is happily married to his wife of more than 25 years and has seven children.

ALSO BY MARTIN WINSLOW

NEW TESTAMENT 260

A 1-Year New Testament Bible Reading Program

Coordinating Musical Downloads Available at

www.nextgenerationfaithfulness.com

PARENTING TIPS FOR THE CHRISTIAN HOME

A Look at Discipleship Methods Within the Home

Includes Practical Tools from Childhood Conversion to College

TRAIN THEM UP: A CHRISTIAN PARENT'S GUIDE TO BALANCING SPORTS AND FAITH

Practical Tips for Families on How to Effectively Disciple Children Involved in Sports

A Challenge to Keep a Living, Vibrant Faith the Number 1 Priority